INNOVATIONS IN INCLUSION:
THE PURDUE
FACULTY & STAFF
DIVERSITY STORY
1997 - 2008

INNOVATIONS
IN
INCLUSION

THE PURDUE FACULTY & STAFF DIVERSITY STORY

1997 - 2008

BARBARA BENEDICT BUNKER

WITH

JANICE EDDY

PURDUE UNIVERSITY PRESS
WEST LAFAYETTE, INDIANA

Library of Congress Cataloging-in-Publication Data

Bunker, Barbara Benedict.
  Innovations in inclusion : the Purdue faculty and staff diversity story,
1997-2008 / Barbara Benedict Bunker and Janice Eddy.
    p. cm.
  ISBN 978-1-55753-528-3
  1. Purdue University. 2. College teachers--Professional relationships--
United States--Case studies. 3. Universities and colleges--United States--
Faculty--Attitudes--Case studies. 4. Multiculturalism--United States--Case
studies. 5. School management and organization--United States--Case studies.
6. Educational innovations--United States--Case studies. I. Eddy, Janice,
1935- II. Title.
LB1778.2.B86 2008
  378.1'2--dc22

                    2008040052

Cover photograph courtesy of Purdue Marketing Communications.

Contents

FOREWORD

SALLY MASON

In June of 2001 I returned, with excitement and some degree of trepidation, to one of my alma maters, Purdue University. The excitement emanated from the recollection of having competed successfully for the job of provost, chief academic officer, of one of our nation's best public research universities. The trepidation came from memories of a graduate education experience that was filled with challenges well beyond those found in the classroom or posed by the curriculum.

Steeped in the land-grant traditions of strong and well-respected agriculture and engineering programs, Purdue University had a reputation for academic rigor and conservatism. Even today, the student body demographic is very different from the typical research university. At Purdue, 40% of the student body is female; at most other major universities, women represent 50% or more of the student body. So, for a woman to be recruited—with enthusiasm—to lead the academic enterprise for Purdue was indeed exciting and different for the institution.

I keep an art poster in my office that quotes the old adage, "Change of any sort requires courage." I arrived at Purdue determined to do my best to grow the faculty, shift the faculty and student demographic, and work on making certain that the chilly climate I experienced as a graduate student was not perpetuated during my tenure or into the future. My early weeks and months on the job gave me much to be optimistic about.

My arrival on campus marked a number of significant milestones. The then new president, Martin Jischke, restructured the senior administration, re-instituting the position of provost, under whose purview were placed all of the key administrative offices essential to our three-pronged mission of learning, discovery, and engagement. We were in the midst of drafting Purdue's first ever strategic plan and gearing up for a major capital campaign, and I knew that significant investments in new programs and faculty positions would be possible. My conversations across the campus also uncovered considerable interest in the campus climate and optimism about what a new administration might be able to effect. In some ways, I walked into the perfect storm. A strong groundwork had been laid, the campus was ready for change, and many were willing to look beyond "the way we've always done it" to ask, "How can we do it better or best?"

From the outset, I took a long view and maintained an interest in effecting evolutionary as opposed to revolutionary change. Some have described what happened at Purdue from 2000 to 2007 as transformational. I hope that history will bear witness that it was also evolutionary, particularly in the progress made in changing the campus climate and growing diversity across all segments of the population.

As you will read in the following pages, this was a labor of love—a team effort, led by many and permeating the entire institution. To the extent possible, and understanding that change is inevitable, we worked to put in place a structure that would live beyond the tenure of one administration. The Diversity Leadership Group (DLG) is now a standing advisory committee to the provost, one through which future provosts can work to develop new initiatives and improve the campus climate for diversity. The capstone event to our development of *Mosaic*, the nickname for our strategic plan for diversity, was a celebration of diversity unlike any seen before at Purdue, in terms of the participants, the activities, and the wonderful meal that were part of our formal evening event.

And despite pressure from many sectors, we continued to make the forums described in this monograph voluntary rather than mandatory. The commitment to this effort is thus strong and enduring, as more and more of our community have chosen to invest their time in the learning and growth opportunities offered by the multicultural and gender forums. Indeed, there is a constant call among those who have attended these forums for more opportunities of similar intensity and design. New hires in many colleges across the campus now receive, as part of their offer letter, a message conveying a positive expectation of attendance at a forum shortly after their arrival on campus.

What you will read in these pages was driven by the optimism and hard work of many fine people. I hold the Purdue community in high esteem for its willingness and commitment to embrace change and dream big. It has been a privilege to be a part of this collective effort.

Sally Mason, President
University of Iowa

INTRODUCTION

BARBARA BENEDICT BUNKER

Over the last ten years, Purdue University has undertaken a culture change initiative that is unprecedented in American higher education. This is the first chapter in the unfolding story of the fundamental shift in campus culture that is required to prepare Purdue's students to act as culturally competent global citizens. An ongoing national discussion about the importance of the learning environment has resulted from the growing diversity in the United States population, the widespread effort of institutions to recruit more underrepresented minorities and international students, and the impact of globalization. American universities' student bodies are increasingly diverse in ethnicity, race, nationality, gender, language, sexual orientation, disability, and religion. At the same time, the faculty and staff, the stable base of the university and the creators of its culture for learning, are much slower to diversify.

The first wave of culture change on campus reflected a general concern about numbers: How do we recruit and retain faculty and students of different backgrounds? As institutions of higher education have begun to increase their numbers, a second and even more important question has emerged: What kind of community is needed to promote and support the learning of students of such diversity and to retain diverse faculty?

1

With leadership changes imminent at Purdue University in spring 2007, it seemed wise to document the ten-year effort to increase the awareness, knowledge, and skills of faculty and staff in the many areas of diversity. This work is unprecedented because it focuses on the faculty and staff in the colleges and schools of the University. The data for this report were gathered by the researcher and author of this document, who interviewed key informants and examined documents, archives, and websites during spring 2007.[1]

What is reported here does not represent the history of diversity at Purdue: There is a long history of recruiting and retaining underrepresented minority students and women (in the more technical fields) that is not covered here. There is also ongoing training and intervention work in the administrative side of the University and in the support units. Many groups and individuals at Purdue have a long history of involvement with issues of diversity and have impacted the campus culture.

This report describes work with faculty and staff in the colleges and schools to change the academic culture so that students, whatever their diversity and gender, will feel welcomed, supported, and included. It begins with the narrative of the ten-year development of this diversity initiative, which includes data on changes that have occurred in the academic culture at Purdue. A section on change in universities and the concepts that underlie the change process concludes the discussion.

The culture change taking place at Purdue is dramatic, although the change process itself is gradual. From a mostly white, very male, Midwestern institution focusing on the sciences and engineering, Purdue is moving toward becoming consciously global. This means creating a welcoming and supportive environment for persons from many cultures, including those within the United States as well as from international communities. This report tells that story: How it started, why it succeeded (when many other institutions have tried and failed), and what is yet to be done.

PART ONE

THE NARRATIVE:
THE
MULTICULTURAL
FORUM

BARBARA BENEDICT BUNKER

THE MULTICULTURAL FORUM

HOW IT ALL BEGAN: 1997

Purdue engineering alumna Deb Grubbe was invited to be the first woman member of the New Directions Chemical Engineering Advisory Board at Purdue. Grubbe had continued her association with Purdue after graduation by returning frequently to speak to the Women in Engineering Program. As a recently promoted director in DuPont Engineering, she came to her first meeting of the New Directions Committee with knowledge of what companies like DuPont were doing to help employees understand workforce diversity and the increasingly global context of business.

The story of that first meeting[2] makes the early issues clear. As she reports it, an item on the agenda at that committee meeting was a report on how some new initiatives were required for chemical engineering. DuPont and other corporations had been supporting minority recruitment efforts in the College of Engineering, but most of the focus was on a summer program to help minority students prepare for academic life at Purdue. To Grubbe, this seemed too narrow a focus: "Why were we only talking about changing the students coming to Purdue, when we should also be focused on changing the environment, the faculty, and the staff? Purdue, to thrive, needed to be able to work with a very diverse group of students." DuPont was providing training to their employees in diversity and needed to reduce the added burden of training graduates they had just hired. They wanted to hire Purdue graduates who already understood the world they were going to be working in and who had the knowledge and skills to be part of that world.

When a request for more funds to support the summer minority program came up on the agenda, Grubbe said clearly, though with much trepidation—since she was the newest, youngest, and only woman committee member—that DuPont would not support such a program unless it also involved new learning for the faculty and staff. This was followed by a long silence, as members of the committee considered what to do. Finally, another member said: "Amoco supports DuPont." After an interval, another voice said: "Exxon supports Amoco and DuPont." At which point, it was clear that they were now in a new ballgame! Something different needed to happen for corporate support to continue, but what?

Engineering needed to prepare graduates to work in a diverse global environment, but faculty could not do that unless they too understood and could be effective in that world. The work needed to begin with the faculty and the staff that supported them and created the culture of engineering. Deb Grubbe proposed that DuPont invite a faculty member to attend a Diversity Workshop at DuPont to gain knowledge of what the corporate world was doing. Nick Delgass, then Associate Head of Chemical Engineering, agreed to go to a workshop in Houston, Texas without really having any idea of what he was getting in to. As he puts it, "My experience was life changing for me!"

Delgass participated in a five day workshop that explored issues of race and gender with a group of male and female DuPont employees who were themselves African American, Hispanic, Asian, and Caucasian. The workshop was led by Janice Eddy and Richard Orange, the external diversity consultants who originated the program at DuPont. In it, he heard the life stories of people whose personal history was totally different from his own, shared his own experiences, engaged in activities, and observed reactions. Through narratives and the sharing of personal experiences, he was able to learn about and experience vicariously some of what women and minorities experience in the workplace that is not generally in the consciousness of those in the mainstream culture. Delgass recalls, "It was absolutely eye opening!"

THE FIRST MULTICULTURAL FORUM

When Delgass returned to campus, it was with a very positive evaluation about the potential of this diversity workshop for engineering. By that time, it was clear that Chemical Engineering alone did not have the numbers or resources to carry out such an undertaking, so the Dean of Engineering, Richard Schwartz, became a key player in decisions about how to go forward. After some negotiation, he agreed to sponsor a pilot Multicultural Forum that was held in Indianapolis in January 1998 from Sunday afternoon through Tuesday evening (2 ½ days). The time frame was planned to accommodate teaching schedules and not take faculty from classes for more than two days. DuPont provided the financial support for this first workshop.

That first Multicultural Forum was planned and facilitated by Janice Eddy, Richard Orange, and Bill Page. There are many forms of diversity training currently being offered in the United States. The Multicultural Forum was designed specifically for Purdue as an educational rather than a confrontational workshop. The stated goals are:

- to increase our cultural competence in preparing students for today's world
- for each of us to take personal responsibility for an environment of inclusion and diversity in our schools and in our lives [3]

Expected Outcomes

What were the general outcomes expected from a program that engaged faculty and staff in a dialogue about race, ethnicity, gender, and sexual orientation? In business organizations, programs often come with expected and specific outcomes or "deliverables." Changing organizational culture to be more knowledgeable, more responsive, and supportive of others with different experiences, values, and ways of doing things is not a deliverable. It is not easily accomplished or quantified. It is a process, sometimes a slow one, often an emergent one, that depends on people being open to new ideas and experiences and willing to consider alternatives to, in this case, "the Purdue way."

The Purdue Culture

Purdue is a highly regarded land-grant university with a long history of proud accomplishments, especially in engineering and the sciences. The "good old boys," as the dominant old culture of Purdue is often captioned, built the University and its reputation as a homogeneous white male culture that was not unlike the cultures of many successful American organizations. As the world outside its doors changed and became more diverse, Purdue worked at recruiting more women and more international and minority students. These students, however, had to find a way to succeed in the old Purdue culture, which was slow to change. Those who did succeed did so with difficulty.

The experience created in the Multicultural Forum engaged faculty and staff in an enlightening dialogue with one another and with students, faculty, and staff of color about diversity. It was hoped that people would discover gaps in their own knowledge that would motivate them to want to know more and to explore and grow. The general outcome expected for all participants at the Multicultural Forum was more knowledge and awareness of what campus life is like for students, faculty, and staff of color, both inside and outside the classroom and with those in their own racial group as well as those in other groups. It included the experiences that minorities were having in the local community where some lived and looked for services. It was expected that the new awareness and knowledge would lead to changes in behavior, specific actions that faculty and staff would take to improve campus life for everyone. It was also expected that the forum experience would help people develop the skills and confidence to move toward and work with others who are different to create a better and more supportive culture. (This same process was expected to occur at the Gender Forums in relation to women.)

Janice Eddy leads a staff of skilled diversity consultants who reflect the diversity of the campus: Barbara Berry, Rosaura Aida

Cepeda, Ann Kusumoto, Bill Page, and Atossa Rahmanifar. They work together in modifying the original forum design as times change and as they receive feedback and suggestions from faculty, staff, and alumni participants. The core activities give information, raise awareness, develop skills, and engage participants in a serious discussion of the academic climate. The brief description of the forum format that follows will give a better feeling for what happens at a typical forum.

Activities During the Multicultural Forum

The Multicultural Forum begins with activities that get people talking with each other about their personal life experiences with difference. Then, over the course of the workshop, information and activities about the history and lived experience of African Americans, Latinos, Asians, Caucasians, Middle Easterners, and Indigenous Americans are presented by the staff (who themselves are members of these groups). After each presentation or activity, the staff facilitates conversations about the information or experience. Participants meet for discussion in two types of groups, one culturally diverse and the other a group of their own culture or ethnicity.

Toward the end of the Multicultural Forum, a panel of alums and advanced students who are participants in that forum talks with the whole group about their student experiences at Purdue and makes recommendations for change. For many faculty members who were interviewed, there was a great deal of new information about the experiences of minorities and women students at Purdue that surprised and sometimes shocked them. Dean Schwartz said about attending the first Multicultural Forum, "The alums talked about their experiences in school which was stressful to hear about. These were recent alums, so it had happened under my watch. It couldn't be talked away and I wasn't aware of it! That really nailed down the urgency of it for me."

TYPICAL RECOMMENDATIONS
FROM MINORITY ALUMNI AND GRADUATE STUDENTS ON THE
FINAL DAY OF THE MULTICULTURAL FORUM

Alumni, graduated in the last ten years:

- You can now try having dialogue with students where you might have been fearful before. We're not offended by you learning to talk about these things. I challenge you to do this.
- Quietness in a student doesn't mean we don't want to be engaged. Be more observant of these students and check in with them, maybe at the end of class.
- Be genuinely curious about your students.
- Don't back away from differences. Say "Oh, that's different, tell me more."
- Be in dialogue. Engage people more and more.
- Find small ways to open up conversation with students who are different.
- Remember that it is hard for "different" students to reach out, so your reciprocating makes a big difference.
- Keep your eyes open for kids falling thru the cracks. After my first exam, if I was struggling, the professors who were most helpful reach out early to help.
- Come to minority programs. It gives minority students hope when faculty show up at events and make relationships—that demonstrates a commitment.
- There should be a required freshman diversity course for all students and it should be expanded with more time for sharing.
- Professors should be aware of the different cultural social and educational experiences and activities

on campus so they can direct people including white students to them.

- Ask yourself, "what would you like others to do for your children abroad?"
- In your classes, speak at the beginning and often about diversity.
- Don't show how surprised you are that I am doing well.
- Don't make "I know what you are going through" statements.
- Don't OVER praise.
- It can get very lonely here.

Advanced graduate students:

- Encourage team projects on the graduate level. One program insisted on three different teams, so people got to know me.
- Don't be so cut and dried. You're not working with robots. We have feelings.
- Mentor students more. Listening is the most important. And introduce students to a whole lot of people.
- Make a personal commitment to be an advocate for students of color.
- There needs to be more nurturing by the professors—more time to talk, to get to know—this is especially true for students of color—it was very hard for me to be just a number here.
- Go beyond work and try to connect at other levels—compliment our lives this way—we will be better students.
- Need to hear "nice job."
- We're glad Purdue made this investment—other diversity courses have been too short or too angry.
- Keep learning after this course.

A Faculty Driven Initiative

As he rode back on the bus from Indianapolis with the first forum group, the dean was impressed to see people kneeling on their seats to talk back and forth with others about what they could do when they got back to campus. He saw the possibility of diversity becoming a faculty-driven effort. So, when a group of his faculty organized an unofficial "Diversity Action Committee," he was supportive. In the fall of 1998, the dean decided to fund and sponsor regular Multicultural Forums for faculty and staff. Since gender was also very important in the College of Engineering, which had had a Women in Engineering Program since 1976, it was also agreed to develop and sponsor a two-day Gender Workshop for graduates of the Multicultural Forum.

From the beginning, everyone acknowledged that attendance at the Multicultural Forums should be voluntary. Faculty members were not likely to appreciate being told to attend. They are always busy with research and teaching, which are their clear priorities, and taking several days off campus for training would not be an easy sell. Based on his own experience, the dean went before his faculty and explained the value and importance of the forums and urged faculty to sign up to attend. Then the dean's office worked informally to encourage heads and other influential faculty who they thought would be opinion leaders to attend. Jeff Wright, an assistant dean of Engineering at that time, and Carolyn Percifield, Director of Corporate Relations and also a member of the dean's staff, were important behind-the-scenes recruiters for the early Multicultural Forums. Marion Blalock, Director of the Minority Recruitment, and Jane Daniels, Director of the Women in Engineering Program, were strong supporters and helped recruit the alums as participants who were crucial to the success of these events.

Inviting, Recruiting, and Influencing Attendance

Each Multicultural Forum was planned for 40-50 in participants, a balance of faculty and staff, men and women, and underrepresented minorities. The Multicultural Forum itself needed to represent the diversity that was being discussed. Getting people to go off cam-

IN THEIR OWN WORDS: JEFF WRIGHT
DEAN OF ENGINEERING, UNIVERSITY OF CALIFORNIA AT MERCED

I came to Purdue in 1982 as a faculty member in the School of Civil Engineering. In 1997, Dick Schwartz, Dean of Engineering, asked me to join his staff half-time as Assistant Dean. We had weekly "cabinet meetings" of the dean's staff and at one of them, Dick announced that we had a request—from an important alum—to participate in a diversity activity. We were all very busy so we looked at each other begrudgingly; was this really essential? Did any of us really have the time? Who could we get to go? It was not at all obvious who should go. We knew that it would be virtually impossible to get senior faculty to go without a clear purpose and potential payoff; we didn't want junior faculty to take the time away from their teaching and research; and we didn't know much about it.

With no gracious way to decline—nobody wanted to tell Deb that we would not be participating—Dick, Larry Huggins, Associate Dean, Carolyn Percifield, Director of Development and Alumni Relations, and I decided to go; at least we'd show up for the first part and duck out when we could.

So we went to the Multicultural Forum in Indianapolis for two-and-a-half days, not knowing what to expect or why we were going off campus. It was an amazing experience! We soon learned that we were not there just to listen, but were "center stage." The workshop was about us, and what a remarkably powerful (to use Carolyn's great word) experience it was. What began as a disjointed and fragmented set of discussions and discourses evolved into an uncomfortable self-realization that behavior results from attitudes, so behavior won't change until attitudes change. My understanding of, and attitudes about, diversity were wrong, and that was not a comfortable place to be.

The message from Richard Orange and the alums of color who participated in the sessions hit me the hardest. It's humbling to learn firsthand of the impact that you are having on others without even knowing it, and depressing to come to the realization that it is not entirely what you intended or wanted. The more I heard, the more I questioned, the more I learned. I'm still learning.

pus for two-and-a-half days was not easy. After the first few years, it was decided to hold the event at a camp nearer to the campus, though not on it, which would enable people to go home at night to their families. This is still the current pattern.

Although much of this report focuses on faculty development, it was early recognized that the staff whose numbers are heavily female are a key resource in creating the climate for students in an academic department. Staff members who were invited had a great deal of contact with students. Often, they had influential roles with regard to schedules, access to jobs, and other important issues in students' lives. They also increased the gender diversity of the early forums. At a more personal level, this was an opportunity for staff members who had not been exposed to diverse life experiences to understand and experience issues relating to diversity. For all these reasons, they were included from the beginning in all forums.

Resistance to attending was plentiful in some quarters. Initially, faculty were skeptical that anything of value would transpire. Some refused to go even when invited by their dean. In business organizations, top management sets expectations and people are expected to conform even if not specifically ordered to do so. People usually read the signals of their superiors and adjust their behavior. In the university, there is a different authority and decision-making structure. The admistration has certain powers, for example, budgetary, the university calendar, and strategic direction. The faculty also has certain powers, for example the curriculum, scholarly pursuits, and faculty recruitment. Autonomy is highly valued by faculty who expect to make most decisions about their work life by themselves. When a dean or department head wants faculty to move in a new direction, offering a compelling rational, enlisting the opinion leaders among the faculty, and gently persuading are more effective than issuing orders. Moreover, the Multicultural Forum is an experience in which people communicate quite personally with each other, which assumes a willingness to engage and a capacity for openness and self-reflection. People who attend voluntarily are more apt to learn from the experience. The dean and associates who were inviting people to participate could speak from their own experience and encourage others to go and make their own judgment. In that first year, many went because their colleagues found it a profound and useful experience. Some faculty members in engineering have never gone. Though they are viewed by some as "needing it the most because they think they don't need it," it is quite clear that required attendance would be counterproductive to learning.

Bumps along the Road

Each Multicultural Forum has its own chemistry produced by the unique set of people who come together. They engage each other and the consulting staff as well as what is going on in the world or on the campus at the time. The consulting staff confer about changes they decide to make based on previous forums and events outside. For example, right after the 9/11 terrorist attack, a unit on Middle Eastern culture was added.

There were, of course, bumps along the road. How they were handled is particularly instructive. At an early forum, a small group of influential faculty had a strong negative reaction to data presented as part of the forum program. They saw it as inaccurate and out of date. They wrote a critical letter to the dean and talked negatively about it to colleagues. As word got around, the credibility of the program was in jeopardy. Faculty members who had had very positive experiences conferred about how to do damage control. They held several luncheons to which they invited potential future attendees and talked openly about what had happened. The faculty who were negative were invited to present their views and talk openly with faculty who found the forums very valuable. They invited people to attend and make their own judgment, which was exactly what happened.

At the same time, the forum staff adjusted and improved the data and materials used in the forums. What may have worked well in a business environment was not always appropriate in an academic setting. New materials and ideas were continually incorporated as the forum staff reviewed each program experience and the participants' feedback. The forum design had an overall flow but was open to new ideas, modifications, and corrective feedback.

> ## IN THEIR OWN WORDS: JACKIE JIMERSON
> ### DIRECTOR OF MULTICULTURAL PROGRAMS, COLLEGE OF PHARMACY, NURSING, AND HEALTH SCIENCES
>
> *What happens after people return from the Multicultural Forums?*
>
> We have postforum lunches with the dean. I am there and I listen. It was a highlight for me to hear faculty talk about what they had learned. One group shared that there were white students in the college that felt that minority students were less capable academically and the faculty challenged that and refuted it, which led to more respect for minority students.
>
> It's good for the dean to hear all this. We then discuss what has been shared and decide what we will do. (Of course, we have a Minority Advocacy Council which is very active in the college also.)

What Happened When Forum Participants Returned to Purdue?

In the College of Engineering, faculty who returned from the forum experience with energy to take some action were encouraged to self-organize and to develop ideas about what to do to create a better learning culture for everyone. They did this in different ways. Some focused on their classrooms and what they could do to make the learning environment more supportive for all students. Steve Beaudoin, Professor of Chemical Engineering, decided to see if he could help the undergraduate students in his core chemical engineering courses get to know each other better and work more collaboratively. He believes that in the working world, the ability to interact effectively with others, including those who are different, is an important skill. He created student project teams that were required to work together to complete assignments that received a group grade. Students participated in several project teams over the course of the semester. Each assignment also included discussion questions that helped them connect with each other by sharing personal experiences. This created a less competitive and more friendly and supportive learning environment. He shared his classroom activities with other faculty in a college-wide workshop and at faculty retreats. This type of innovation has been sustained, as over the past two years, two faculty who are members of the Diversity Action Committee have been working with the freshman engineering course to create a more personal and cooperative environment.

As faculty returned from the Multicultural Forums, some did make changes in the way they taught that they felt were responsive to what they had learned, but there was not easily accessible structured help for faculty who were motivated to make changes in their classroom teaching style but were not sure how to go about it. Others took action by helping with recruiting and outreach in the Minority Engineering Program.

Collective Action

An informal group of faculty began to meet to develop both short-range and long-range ideas for change in the college and its structures. For example, at that time there were very few women on the engineering faculty, and female candidates seldom were presented by search committees. It was proposed that the informal faculty group (who later became official as the Diversity Action Committee) review and interview all candidates for deans or heads about their views on diversity. Some of the members of this ad hoc group also began to be selected for search committees so that general awareness of the value of having more women faculty and a willingness to look for them grew. When the Multicultural Forum began there were 17 women faculty (three full professors) in an Engineering faculty of 267. In June 2007, there were 38 women faculty (total faculty 307). Now, there are eight full professors, seven associate professors and 20 assistant professors.

In 2002, Linda Katehi became the new Dean of Engineering. Initially, as she got to know the College of Engineering, she did not take a strong position favoring or not favoring the forums. This meant that administration and faculty who believed in the importance of the forums worked hard during the transition period to maintain the positive momentum. In 2003, the dean attended the Multicultural Forum at the same time as the new provost, Sally Mason. Both women had very good experiences at the forum and Katahi became a strong supporter of them. While she was dean, her associate deans and staff included women and minorities. She made decisions that signaled the importance of including more women candidates in the faculty search and interview process. The number of women faculty increased under her leadership. In 2004, Dean Katehi was hired away from Purdue and after a national search, Dr. Leah Jamieson, Purdue faculty member since 1976, was selected as the new dean, the second woman dean of Engineering, which is unprecedented in the United States. In 2007, Dr. France A. Córdova was hired as the new president of Purdue University, one of the first woman presidents of a major technical university in the United States and a strong and clear signal about the direction of the University.

Student Diversity

The College of Engineering had recruiting programs and had been working on increasing the student diversity of underrepresented minorities in the school since the 1970s. Marion Blalock directed this program for thirty years, which not only reached out to high schools and brought students to campus to experience what engineering would be like as a career, but also worked with students when they were on campus to create a supportive environment that would help them succeed. Other campuses used Purdue as a model and instituted similar programs. But according to several faculty interviewed, the pedagogy of the classroom did not change very much to accommodate the different learning styles that vary across all students, including minorities.

What Counts for Promotion?

There have also been changes in the promotion and tenure process. One woman who was on the engineering faculty before the forums started and who has been active in diversity issues since she arrived at Purdue talked about her two experiences assembling her dossier for promotion. When she was first considered for tenure, her activities on behalf of women were not valued and she was not encouraged to include them in her dossier as part of her service to the University. That early climate, she said, "interfered with my productivity." More recently, when she prepared credentials for promotion from associate to full professor, these activities were included as part of the package of valuable activities she had contributed.

Impact Outside of Purdue

Faculty does leave Purdue for better or different roles during their academic careers. Jeff Wright was recruited from his role as associate dean of Engineering at Purdue to be the new dean of Engineering in the all new tenth campus of the University of California at Merced. At Purdue, he was one of the first to attend a Multicultural Forum with others from the dean's office. When he went, he didn't know what to expect. He describes it as an amazing experience. "I really had an awakening. I had to pay attention to this because it was affecting what I did whether I knew it or not." He realized that there were complex issues to be understood and that included understanding his own background and behavior first, before he could understand how what he does influences others. As an associate dean in Engineering at Purdue, he was part of the team that recruited faculty for the Multicultural Forums and worked with the beginnings of the Diversity Action Committee. When he moved to UC Merced, he realized that rather than trying to shape a university with a 100 year history, he was working with a clean slate to begin with. As a result, the cornerstones of the new campus at Merced include strong values about diversity, inclusiveness, and representation. Jeff Wright realized the importance of establishing, from the outset, a culture in this new university that values diversity. He has recruited a wonderfully diverse faculty and student body in terms of both representation and attitudes, and credits his success in large part to his experience with the Multicultural Forum at Purdue in the College of Engineering. This ripple effect, like the stone thrown in a pond, can have impact outside the university as faculty change jobs, attend meetings, and talk with colleagues.

THE INITIATIVE SPREADS: THE COLLEGE OF SCIENCE AND THE COLLEGE OF AGRICULTURE CO-SPONSOR FORUMS

Word gets around. Other faculty and administrators in colleges with common interests heard about the forums and expressed curiosity. Engineering had invited individual faculty from Science and Agriculture who were teaching engineering students to participate. Harry Morrison, then Dean of the College of Science, attended a forum with associates from his office. All were very positive about their experience and decided the College of Science should encourage participation in the forums. A similar process occurred in the College of Agriculture. Dick Schwartz, Dean of Engineering, spoke positively about the forums to Vic Lechtenberg, Dean of the College of Agriculture, who sent a few faculty members. When they returned with positive reports, he decided the college should be involved. Science and Agriculture cosponsored one forum a semester, from spring 2002 until fall 2003, when a three-way sponsorship, including engineering, began. Until that time, Engineering had sponsored one forum each semester from 1998.

In the new cosponsorship, inviting faculty and staff was initiated from the Dean's office, but each college had to recruit a few alums or advanced students for the final morning's panel on the Purdue culture as experienced by students. These women and minorities play a critical role in the panel on the final day and are a key element in the success of each forum. Finding, recruiting, and preparing them is a delicate and time-consuming job that was part of Barbara Clark's role in the College of Science and Professor Ron Coolbaugh's role in the College of Agriculture.

The College Of Science

Histories with regard to diversity are interestingly different from college to college. The College of Science had grant-supported innovative programs for Women in Science focused on student retention and mentoring from the mid-1970s. Dean Harry Morrison appointed Barbara Clark Director of the Women in Science Programs in 1997. Her work focused on working with faculty on classroom climate and with mentoring programs. At the same time, the Dean began meeting with all the women faculty to discuss their concerns. Associate Dean Martha Chiscon, developer of the Women in Science Program and a strong faculty voice for women's needs, influenced Morrison to meet with the women faculty once every semester. In these discussions, it became clear that recruiting more women to the faculty was a priority and Dean Morrison directed that there should be a woman on every search committee. Although not all women faculty agreed with this decision, they began to understand its usefulness as they were able to raise questions about the criteria used for not considering some candidates' applications. Over the years, the number of women faculty in science departments has indeed increased (See Appendix A, Table 2).

What Happened When Forum Participants Returned?

The learning and impact of the Multicultural Forums occurs at the personal level. People return from the forums and decide what actions are appropriate for them to take. In Science, some faculty made changes in the way they structured or taught their classrooms. For example, they gave more thought to how they assigned lab pairings. Across the college, there was a great effort to recruit more women and minorities. Using the College of Engineering as the model, the College of Science also established The Faculty Committee for Diversity at the college level. When they interview candidates, every position from head of department and above is interviewed by this committee and the results are reported to the dean and the search committee. The scale runs from *excellent* as regards their understanding of diversity through *may need to raise their awareness* by going to a forum to *unacceptable*. This sends a clear message to candidates about the importance of this issue to the leadership of the college.

Improving the Student Experience

When Jeff Vitter, Dean of Science (2002-08), was hired, he attended a Multicultural Forum where he was deeply impacted by minority students talking about their traumatic freshman year experience living in the residence halls. He decided to do something about it, so he asked Barbara Clark to take the lead and develop a program that would help students respect and value differences as they found them in their living units. Working with a group of diversity directors, the LEAD program trained student leaders how to do values clarification workshops, which they led in the residence halls. After a successful one-year pilot, the program is now supported out of the Diversity Resource Office.

Increased sensitivity to issues of diversity also led to concern about graduate women and minority students who were not getting timely information about how they were progressing in their programs. Apparently, some faculty members were hesitant, and perhaps uncomfortable, about giving clear feedback to those of a different race or gender. This led to a policy change that now mandates annual feedback from faculty to graduate students so that students know where they stand.

The Core Curriculum

The College of Science has also been working for almost two years on a revision of its core curriculum requirements. This was the first revision of the core in over forty years. The idea was to revise the core requirements in line with what students need in the twenty-first century. This curriculum revision passed after more than a year of discussion and debate in May 2007. It includes Language and Culture as one of the core learning areas. Students must take either a course on diversity, study a language, or enroll in a study abroad experience.

Diversity and the West Lafayette Community

The forums also raised awareness of the difficulty that minorities and particularly people of color have had buying or renting housing and finding the services and products they need in the community. This community situation, among other factors, has made recruiting minority faculty difficult. As this awareness has grown across the campus, influential members of the larger community have been invited to participate in the forums.

The College of Agriculture

In the College of Agriculture, the student body began to include more women in the 1980s and 1990s, but the faculty was still predominantly white and male. Today, about 46.2% of students in the college are women. Dean Victor Lechtenberg became aware of the discrepancy between the student and faculty populations and encouraged Suzanne Neilsen, a tenured woman faculty member, to convene a women's faculty group to make recommendations to the dean about issues regarding the current climate for women faculty and recruiting more faculty women. He promised to be available to the group and to provide whatever support they needed. This group first convened before Agriculture began to participate in either the Multicultural Forum or the Gender Forum and is still active. They meet both for social support and to discuss issues that affect women differently than men, for example, slowing down the tenure clock for women having babies, effective mentorship of younger women faculty, dealing with perceived lack of respect, and the demands of extension work on women with families. They meet with the dean at least once a year and they also interview candidates and have input into administrative hiring decisions.

Janice Eddy met with the women faculty in Agriculture as she did in Science and Engineering and has been an occasional consultant to each dean about issues women are facing. About gender, one woman faculty member commented: "My [male] colleagues had a harder time [at the Gender Forum] accepting some of the ideas of inequality though they also told me it helped to hear our side of the story. Most faculty think there is no problem."

As in Engineering, the dean attended the first cosponsored Multicultural Forum himself and was present to kick off the opening of subsequent forums. It is very clear from many comments across the colleges that the deans' clear leadership and support sends the message that the Multicultural Forums are important to the college. This has impact on people's interest and willingness to make the time to attend. The invitation to attend a forum comes directly from the dean.

Understanding the Experience of Minorities and Women

Several respondents from Agriculture who attended the forums spoke of learning a great deal about the isolation and difficulties that minority faculty and students experience in the predominantly Eurocentric culture of Purdue. Minority faculty described their loneli-

---

IN THEIR OWN WORDS: JEFF WRIGHT
DEAN OF ENGINEERING, UNIVERSITY OF CALIFORNIA
AT MERCED

Getting faculty to do anything is difficult; getting faculty to attend the Multicultural Forums was painful. In my experience, faculty members generally want to do the right thing, certainly as it relates to students success and scholarship. But this means different things to different faculty. Most everyone agrees that research and education are number one and number two. And 99% agree we need a good community within engineering, but they measure it differently. Engineers are problem solvers, and diversity within the Schools was not perceived as problematic. After all, Purdue had the best programs in the nation for minority engineering education (we had Marion Blalock) and the best program in the nation for women in engineering (we had Jane Daniels)! Faculty generally felt they were doing just fine: "Diversity is not a problem for us so let's go on to something important!"

We decided early on that in order to really get this going to the extent that it would take hold and really have an impact we would have to 1) somehow keep this as a voluntary activity for the faculty, and 2) somehow get the true opinion leaders from within the ranks of the faculty to volunteer. We had our work cut out for us; getting very smart people who were extremely busy to carve out substantial time away from campus to do something that we couldn't really describe, but that would help address a problem that they were convinced didn't exist.

Carolyn and I spent many hours—initially over coffee, then later over beer—wondering if this could ever be successful, and trying to remember how we got ourselves into this situation.

ness and isolation and lack of inclusion in the community. Others spoke about their desire to take action toward making the culture more inclusive but accepting that there was no structured way to do that. There are differing reactions to the Multicultural Forums among faculty and staff (see "Ongoing Evaluation of the Multicultural Forums," below) and several people pointed out that the lack of structured follow-up missed an opportunity to keep people engaged and thinking about these issues. Before sponsoring Multicultural Forums, the college had a diversity director whose work was primarily student recruitment and retention. Efforts to increase minority enrollment were made over the years, but retention depends in part on a supportive climate. The forums helped faculty and staff understand what was missing that needed attention.

Faculty Initiatives

A faculty committee called the Diversity Action Team in Agriculture (DATA) was created in the early 2000s by the dean to consider what could be done to promote an appreciation of diversity. Among the early projects was consultation with the curriculum committee to create a requirement for a course in diversity. After several years of work, the college voted that all students beginning in fall 2007 would be required to take one multicultural course. The course, "Communicating across Cultures," includes content about all types of diversity with an accompanying lab run by faculty plus participation in a community project. Other courses are also identified and can meet this requirement. Agriculture was the second college, after Liberal Arts, to make diversity a core requirement.

DATA completed a college-wide survey of attitudes in 2006 and is developing a final report that will serve as a baseline for the college. They also interview candidates for leadership posts in the college. They have been positively affected by the University-wide change in the membership of Promotion and Tenure Committees so that associate professors vote in tenure decisions for assistant professors. This has brought more diversity to the promotion process and helped more people understand the process. They are discussing potential bias in student evaluations of women and minority faculty that may affect the promotion process. In other words, they are looking at institutional practices and policies for inadvertent or implicit discrimination.

What went on in Agriculture was specific to that college, but it was not isolated from what was happening in other colleges. As Engineering put in place some of its faculty initiatives, other faculty heard about what was happening there and ideas spread, especially between Engineering, Agriculture, and Science, which have many overlapping interests and relationships. In addition, when President Jischke arrived on the campus in 2001 and made diversity a key part of his strategic plan for the University, there was reinforcement from the top of the organization for moving forward with diversity initiatives.

More Bumps along the Road and Resistance

At a forum that took place just as the colleges of Engineering, Science, and Agriculture began cosponsoring the forums, a small group of department heads and faculty decided that they had learned enough and that the forums were too long, and they left early. This was upsetting to some faculty and staff who were attending and impacted the remaining group. The new provost also heard about this incident and spoke to all the deans and department heads at a university-wide meeting about it. She expressed her displeasure that these leaders were not supporting the diversity initiative and made it clear that it was time well spent for university leaders to support the Multicultural Forums. This also sent a very clear message about the kind of support from the top that the forums had.

Faculty Resistance

But what of the faculty that choose not to attend the Multicultural Forum, even when invited by their dean? In all three colleges, there are a group of white, male, older professors who have chosen not to attend. Since this is a voluntary activity, they continue to be invited, but I have the sense that most proponents of this experience have given up hope that they will change their minds. They tend to be older faculty who are moving toward retirement. At the same time, new faculty are being hired and Science has adopted Engineering's offer letter that includes a paragraph about the Multicultural Forum and tells new faculty that they are expected to attend a forum within their first two years at Purdue. Agriculture strongly encourages new faculty to attend. As new faculty participate and older faculty retire, it is assumed that a critical mass will eventually have had this important experience.

THE FORUMS EXPAND TO INCLUDE ALL THE COLLEGES

In the fall of 2003, Dean Vitter of the College of Science invited the new provost, Sally Mason, a biologist, to attend one of the Multicultural Forums. When Provost Mason was a graduate student at Purdue, she experienced the culture and climate as discouraging to women in science. She was very concerned as provost to assess the situation and take initiative to create a welcoming culture for women and minorities throughout the University.

The New Provost Takes the Helm

Sally Mason had a good experience at the forum she attended. She said that she learned a lot and she enjoyed it because it provided a structure for thinking and real conversation about important issues. It fit with her agenda as provost: "How do you move an institution that has been around a long time and is steeped in tradition? How can it be moved to be more responsive to its people." Several people who attended that forum commented appreciatively that the new provost participated just the way everyone else did. In fact, several people didn't know what her role was until toward the end of the event. The new dean of Engineering, Linda Katehi, was a participant in the same forum.

The new provost had conversations with Janice Eddy and was impressed with her expertise in the diversity area as well as her passion for what she was doing. Her own experience confirmed that the Multicultural Forums would move Purdue forward. She met with Eddy and developed a plan for expanding the forums to all the colleges, which happened gradually over the next several years. The Provost agreed to pick up 50% of the forum costs from her budget.

This meant that the financial strain of supporting the forums in each college was considerably reduced. She also hired Barbara Clark of the College of Science one-quarter time to administer the forums.

In the 2004-2005 academic year, three schools and colleges, Technology, Veterinary Medicine, and Management, began participating in a Multicultural Forum coordinated through the Provost's Office. Then, in 2005-2006, the other four colleges, Liberal Arts, Consumer and Family Sciences, Education, and Pharmacy, Nursing, and Health Sciences, joined together to participate in the forum so that two or three forums were now scheduled each semester. Parallel to this schedule, one Gender Forum has been offered each semester since fall 2004, with two scheduled per semester beginning fall 2007.

Diversity and the Larger Community

At the alumni and student panel reflecting on experiences at Purdue that occurs on the last day of the Multicultural Forum, experiences, issues, and concerns that are raised often go beyond a specific department, school, or college to the wider campus. Since this is all part of the culture that supports learning, some persons who support academics have been invited to the forums so that they, too, can understand issues of diversity. Over several years, members of the campus and West Lafayette police, enrollment management, student services, the libraries, sports and recreation center, student health center, and financial aid have all participated. In July 2007, the first summer forum was scheduled, which included many people from these groups, since summer is an easier time for them to participate. In addition, there has been an effort to reach out to the larger community of West Lafayette, since diversity issues occur in off-campus housing and interactions with services in the community. The mayor and representatives from the mayor's office as well as key business leaders have participated.

Technology, Veterinary Medicine, and Management

The College of Technology, the School of Veterinary Medicine, and the School of Management began cosponsoring forums in 2004.

They were the first three colleges in the process of including the whole University that occurred after Provost Sally Mason agreed to pay 50% of the Multicultural Forum's budget.

The College of Technology

The College of Technology is a young college by Purdue standards, only 45 years old, but the third largest college with programs in ten locations around Indiana as well as on the West Lafayette Campus. It offers programs in applied technology including aviation, computers, industrial, manufacturing, and building construction, to mention only a few. Its faculty and administration historically have had few women and minorities. The current Dean, Dennis Depew, returned to Purdue in 2002 just as the new provost, Sally Mason, was hired. He said, "Sally is the first female provost, and you can't underestimate the power of that. In my first 14 years at Purdue, there was one female dean and that was in Education. My reaction was 'Wow, this biologist from Kansas is going to be the Provost.' The message that sent was big news!"

Dean Depew charted a clear course for the college beginning with gender diversity. He diversified his own office by hiring a woman as associate dean. He encouraged diversity in the candidate pools to the point that currently all eight departments have women on the faculty. In technology 16.1% of tenure-track faculty are women. There has also been an increase in diversity among tenure-track faculty over the last ten years (from .7% to 8.7%) The dean has made clear to department heads that diversity is a university priority. Letters of invitation to the forums invite people to attend on behalf of the dean and their department head. Like all other deans, he is present at the beginning of every forum to signal its importance and encourage his faculty and staff to open themselves to this kind of learning.

The School of Veterinary Medicine

The School of Veterinary Medicine is moving steadily toward becoming much more diverse. Women are enrolling in veterinary medicine programs in great numbers, so that the student body is

84.5% female. The number of women faculty has almost doubled over the last ten years. They are now 28.6% of the tenured faculty. There are slightly more female than male adjunct faculty members. The college has also made significant progress in attracting African American and Asian faculty. The dean is African American. Veterinary Medicine encourages students to get experience abroad for five or six weeks in their senior year. The dean's office supplements the cost of this experience.

The Multicultural Forums are viewed as assisting faculty and staff in the process of creating an hospitable culture that supports learning for all. Faculty are encouraged to attend by their department heads and the leadership of the school.

The Krannert School of Management

The Krannert School of Management has had a mixed history with the Multicultural Forums. Initially faculty reactions were lukewarm. The diversity director was asked to develop a more cognitive and business case-oriented approach; it was offered as short workshops on Fridays. These ran for several years with mixed reviews. With the departure of the person in that role, a new diversity director has been hired. It is too soon to know the direction this person will take. Management will likely continue sending some faculty and staff to the forums.

Management tenure-track faculty is 33.7% minority, of which 16.9% is international, and both represent increases over a ten-year period. There are 19.1% women among tenure-track faculty, which represents a gradual increase over the last ten years.

The Final Four: Liberal Arts, Consumer and Family Sciences, Education, and Pharmacy, Nursing, and Health Sciences

The final group of colleges began their participation in 2005-2006, so their experience with the forums is relatively recent. Generally, these colleges all have more women faculty than most of the other more technical collages. They are diverse with regard to gender though not with regard to underrepresented minorities. Three colleges have some faculty whose research and expertise is in the area of diversity.

In the colleges that were the first to participate, most people had no idea what to expect. They got the message from the leadership that this was important and from participants that they had had a good experience, and so they went. In this final group, the faculty familiar with work on diversity may have expected a more academic conference with the latest research on diversity issues and did not anticipate the personal growth experience. For some, it was eye opening and very positive. Others focused on presentations that they felt were dated and did not represent the best of current thinking. The forum staff has accepted this feedback and made changes in some presentations. Every college has its own culture and the forum staff make adjustments in design as they interact with participants and develop an understanding of the issues. One person raised the interesting issue of "how Purdue might tap the smart people on the faculty who study racism and diversity to help."

The College of Liberal Arts

The College of Liberal Arts is a large college with ten departments. Women tenure-track faculty are 38.3% of the faculty and tenure-track minorities are 14.8%, with both increasing gradually over the last ten years. The dean invites faculty and staff personally to attend the forums and expects his department heads to also be champions. He believes that it is becoming accepted that this is an important thing to do and that resistance and nonparticipation are not acceptable. The colleges differ in whether they choose to put attendance at a forum as part of the offer letter to new faculty. Liberal Arts does not, but the college norms support attending

The College of Consumer and Family Sciences

The College of Consumer and Family Sciences prepares students who will manage in business and in the hospitality industry. They expect to work with very diverse populations, so that there has been an emphasis on multicultural activities in the college. A number of students go abroad for part of their training. Since its founding as a college of home economics, there is a history of women's leadership and a predominantly female faculty. In fact, an important diversity issue in the college has been to include more men on the faculty and balance the genders. Consistent with this intention, the tenure-track faculty is 41.8% women, which is less than ten years ago. Minorities constitute 20% of tenure-track faculty and 5.5% of these are international.

The process of involving faculty in the forums is similar to other colleges already described. In addition, there are multicultural committees in the college that people can volunteer for.

The College of Education

The College of Education has 56.7% tenure-track faculty who are women. That percentage has increased gradually over the last ten years. There are equal numbers of men and women at the full professor level and more women than men as associate or assistant professors. There are 8.3% minority tenure-track faculty, almost exclusively at the assistant professor level. Two areas of the college have research and scholarly interests in multicultural studies, Curriculum and Cultural Foundations. The college is working to attract more African American and Latino students. They have some programs abroad and are becoming more international in their faculty.

There is some resistance to attending by those who think they already know this area. The dean strongly supports people going and sees it as a good experience. Like many others, he is concerned that there be more follow-up back in the college and wonders if better use could be made of the resources within Purdue.

The College of Pharmacy, Nursing, and Health Sciences

The College of Pharmacy, Nursing, and Health Sciences Minority tenure-track faculty has doubled over a ten-year period with currently 15.2% of the tenure-track faculty being minority. There is a minority advocacy committee composed of faculty and staff that advises the dean. There is active work supporting minority students who enroll in the college and creating opportunities for them to interact informally with faculty. As a result, their student graduation rate is outstanding.

About 30% of the tenure-track faculty are women, which is a decrease from 39.8% ten years ago. Women are primarily at the associate and assistant professor level and not in leadership roles.

When people return from the Multicultural Forum, the dean has a lunch meeting with them to hear about their experience and what they are bringing back to the college. The Diversity Director, Jackie Jimerson, sits in on these meetings. Action plans develop at these meetings, which she can assist as they develop. This model of follow-up has been quite successful in Pharmacy. Other colleges are considering it as a way of developing their own implementation plans.

THE NUMBERS

From 1998 to the end of 2008, 671 engineering faculty, staff, alumni, and advanced students have attended the Multicultural and the Gender Forums. More specifically, 415 engineering faculty have attended the Multicultural Forum and 256 faculty have attended the Gender Forum. The College of Agriculture has sent a total of 365 faculty, staff, alumni, and student participants. The College of Science has sent 291 persons. Three colleges began sending people in 2004 and their numbers are now growing. The College of Techology has sent 140 participants. The School of Veterinary Medicine has sent 139 participants. The Krannert School of Management has sent 63 participants. The colleges that are the most recent participants have numbers near 100 each. The total number of persons attending forums as of December 2008 was 2,417.

ONGOING EVALUATION OF THE MULTICULTURAL FORUMS

Feedback from participants is collected at the end of each forum and used by the consulting staff to assess what is going well and what needs revision. These forms also include personal feedback to each consulting staff member and an overall reaction to the forum in the form of the question: "Would you recommend this forum to others?" The year 2006 was selected as a sample year to review the evaluations because all of the colleges were participating in the forums by that time. In 2006, there were six forums and data from 224 participants. Of this group, only six participants (2.7%) said they would not recommend it while 197 (87.9%) said they would. Twenty-one people (9.3%) were uncertain and said "Maybe."

In an earlier study of the first five years of Multicultural Forums in the College of Engineering[4], Klod Kokini, Professor of Mechanical Engineering and Associate Dean for Academic Affairs, and some colleagues collected data from previous participants (53% response rate) and found that:

- 91% of previous participants "rated the overall quality of the forum good, very good, or excellent"
- 91% of forum participants would recommend the forum for engineering faculty
- 88% would recommend the forum for engineering staff
- 75% had actually recommended it to someone

They asked respondents to assess retrospectively their state before and after the forum experience. Specifically, they were interested in an affective component, that is, positive and negative feelings; a behavioral component, that is, intention to act and actual behaviors; and a cognitive component, that is, knowledge and beliefs. They believe that these are the components that mobilize people as "diversity agents." They found:

- Significantly better understanding/awareness of diversity issues
- Significantly more involved in diversity related activities
- more positive and less negative toward diversity issues
- mixed emotions involving both benefits and costs emotionally to raising awareness

In fall 2006, Kevin Kelly, Professor and Head of the Department of Educational Studies, and Nadine Dolby, Associate Professor in Curriculum and Instruction, did a more rigorous qualitative and a quantitative evaluation of the Multicultural Forums. They had both preforum and postforum measures for each participant. They found that the forums raised awareness "that members of diverse groups

IN THEIR OWN WORDS: TONI MUNGUIA
DIVERSITY DIRECTOR, THE COLLEGE OF TECHNOLOGY

As a result of participating in the Multicultural Forums, there's an awareness of the importance of diversity and its importance to the College and the University. I get support from faculty when I ask for help with my programs.

I have seen some progress but we have a long way to go. The administration is really trying to bring this issue to the forefront. When I came here 12 years ago, the Latino population was small. There was no Latino Cultural Center and no organized Latino voice. When students say "We never see any change," my response is that you don't see change in one student generation, but I have seen Latino organizations come together and have a voice that led to the Latino Cultural Center. I was able to tell students about that. I encourage them if they have an idea and something they are passionate about to speak up to the administration and bring it as far as they can before they graduate. It takes time.

still experience the harmful effects of discrimination and stereotyping (at Purdue)" (p. 3) and that the quality of conversation regarding diversity at the forums was experienced as valuable. They also found that the action plans that many participants reported developing immediately after the forum faded from the memory of many participants over time. They did not ask about institutional changes that the forums might have stimulated nor about other changes that were not "action plans."[5]

The question, "What are the outcomes of these forums?" is an important one. Once a person has attended a forum, there are various levels at which change can occur. People who have expanded their knowledge and appreciation of others from different backgrounds may interact differently, speak out when they hear others devalue or stereotype others, or behave differently in their classroom or place of work. Most of the research on outcomes has focused at this level. However, forum graduates in roles where they have power or influence have opportunities to become agents of change, as we have seen in the leadership of the "early adopters" in the Colleges of Engineering, Agriculture, and Science as well as in the Provost's role. This report documents some of the changes that have occurred in the University's organizational fabric, in policy and structure, which in turn impacts the culture and is the context that shapes individual behavior.

Institutional change also occurs through informal channels, as people interact, and through the contagious spread of good ideas. People talk to each other and hear about practices that others are adopting that produce good results. In the business world, this is often referred to as "best practices" or "benchmarking." The sharing that occurs at the forums, where three or four colleges are together for several days, including informal occasions like meals and coffee breaks, makes this kind of contagion of ideas even more likely. A number of practices that started in the College of Engineering, including the interventions in the way faculty searches are conducted, invitations to the forums for new faculty, and the establishment of diversity action committees have spread across the campus. By 2007, all the colleges had someone in the role of diversity director. This role includes the important work of recruiting and retaining women and minority students, but has expanded to include other diversity related initiatives. Diversity directors are active members of the dean's staff in many schools and colleges. The active personal involvement of the deans in supporting faculty action, in making sure that faculty who rose to leadership positions also support diversity initiatives, and in appointing diversity directors to their staffs sent a clear message. Some changes did not result immediately from forum participation but emerged over time as people continued to talk about diversity issues and invented new ways to work on them. The strong messages and actions from President Jischke and Provost Mason during this period made diversity a salient issue for everyone at Purdue. Many respondents that I interviewed spoke about the importance of leadership from the top in enabling them to take action.

At the same time, it is clear that for many respondents, there needs to be more structured support for implementation of plans and ideas after the forums. The college of Pharmacy's post-forum meetings provide an important new structure, but there seems to be a general agreement that more could be done to support implementation.

PART TWO

THE NARRATIVE: DEVELOPING THE GENDER FORUM

BARBARA BENEDICT BUNKER

DEVELOPING THE GENDER FORUM

The five-day DuPont Diversity Workshop dealt with both multi-cultural and gender issues. A five-day workshop at Purdue was not seen as feasible for faculty or staff, so it was agreed to deal with multicultural issues in the Multicultural Forum and to develop the Gender Forum subsequently. Although the College of Engineering has a strong history of activities recruiting women students, the number of women faculty and women in leadership roles has, as we have indicated, been low until fairly recently. The Gender Forum was developed after the Multicultural Forums because Janice Eddy believes that work on race and ethnicity should precede work on gender and prepares people for it. Therefore, candidates for a gender workshop needed to have already attended a Multicultural Forum.

A Short History of Women in Engineering

The College of Engineering has a very long history of nationally recognized innovation in programs for women in engineering that date back to 1969, when they began focusing attention on recruiting more women undergraduates. In the late 1970s, Jane Daniels was hired as director of the Women in Engineering Program. In her more than 20 years in that role, she and her associates not only recruited more women but were the leading-edge creators of programs (with the help of grants from foundations like Sloan and NSF) that helped retain the women who enrolled. These programs included mentoring, building a supportive community through housing, and working with faculty and teaching assistants to create a classroom environment that encouraged the participation of women and others who find the traditional competitive classroom difficult to navigate.

The last project, the Interactive Theater Project, was a popular workshop in which actors demonstrated how very small changes in faculty behavior can create a different environment for women in the classroom. For example, when asking a question of the class, an instructor, rather than recognizing the first person whose hand goes up, might pause for five seconds or so to allow everyone to think and then raise their hands if they want to respond, and then pick from all the raised hands. The workshop was very well received on campus and spread from Engineering to other schools and colleges. The project got national attention and so much publicity for Purdue that Daniels was overwhelmed by calls from other campuses to know more about what they were doing.

Her response was to collaborate with the few other universities that were also creating experimental programs to recruit and retain women engineering students and sponsor a national conference where colleges and universities could network, share information, and build on what was being learned. The first conference in 1990 led to the formation of a national organization, Women in Engineering Programs and Advocates, Inc. (WEPAN). From a once-a-year conference, WEPAN has become a strong nonprofit national association promoting innovation, disseminating materials, and providing training.

Retention of women students improved dramatically. The number of women that enrolled at Purdue and nationally increased until the mid 1980s and then held steady at about 20%. This phenomenon, which is also found in science, is seen as a national concern, and the National Science Foundation is currently sponsoring a program of major grants that will innovate in the way these disciplines are taught in colleges and universities.

In contrast, the recruitment and promotion of women faculty has improved gradually over the years and more dramatically since 2001 (see Appendix A). There have always been significant numbers of women staff and this continues to be the case.

The First Gender Forum

Since Janice Eddy and her colleague Bill Page were planning the work tailored to the Purdue situation, they had to learn about and understand the history and culture in which women were working. The first Gender Forum in 1999 brought together men and women faculty and staff to explore gender issues. The women faculty who came did not feel comfortable talking with their male colleagues about their histories as women faculty at Purdue. What in some cases was a very isolating and painful set of career experiences was just too painful to resurrect. For example, they may have been told some version of "You are never going to make it at Purdue. It's a man's world here," or, "If you keep speaking up, the good old boys will get you."

That first forum did not go well. Janice Eddy, who is a pioneer in gender work in organizations, took this to mean that she needed to take another approach. It was clear that a different design for the event was needed.

The Two Day Retreat: Faculty Women in Engineering

Eddy decided to interview the women engineering faculty, which she did either individually or in small groups. She discovered that they did not know each other very well nor had they explored their common concerns. Dean Schwartz approved and funded her proposal for a two-day off-campus retreat for women faculty in engineering in September 1999. Leah Jamieson, a senior woman faculty member at that time, took leadership in encouraging women to attend. The retreat was organized around three agenda themes:

1. After getting to know each other's situation, what kinds of support might you provide each other?
2. How will you mentor the new faculty women being hired?
3. What contribution do you want to make as women faculty to the College of Engineering?

Telling Her Story

An important component of the retreat was the sharing of the history and experiences of these faculty women. Gradually, women told each other their career stories as they related to gender. For many, it was a painful experience; for some, it was cathartic. Most had never told any other colleague about these experiences. They had borne them in isolation. Discovering that they were not alone and that others also had had difficult experiences was amazing to some and created a sense of support and camaraderie among those present. They laughed, they cried, and they helped Janice Eddy think about how to include other women faculty and staff and their male colleagues in a Gender Forum that would be helpful to everyone.

Recruiting More Women Faculty

Consideration of the idea of making a contribution to the College of Engineering led to an animated discussion about faculty search practices and ideas about influencing the search process in order to increase the number of women candidates who were brought to

IN THEIR OWN WORDS: DENNIS DEPEW
DEAN OF THE COLLEGE OF TECHNOLOGY

I was a faculty member here until 1999 when I took a job at another university as Assistant Dean of the Graduate School. I returned to Purdue in 2002 as one of the first deans hired by the new provost, Sally Mason. Our college had existed for 40 years with very few women faculty and no women deans. The strategic plan of President Jischke emphasized improving diversity of the faculty, staff, and students. I started by promoting gender diversity: I hired a female associate dean and we have markedly increased the number of women and minority faculty.

This administration is the first time that minority communities had someone who listened and wanted to march with them. Previously, we had projects and programs, but not leadership who put their full weight and power into it. Sally Mason was the first female provost, and you can't underestimate the power of that. In my first 14 years at Purdue, there was one female dean and that was in Education. My reaction to the new provost was, "Wow, this biologist from Kansas is going to be provost!" The message this sent was big news. President Jischke set out to do that and I wanted to do the same thing in my own college. You don't tread water in higher education. You are either moving forward or you are losing ground.

campus for interviews. The group met several times after the off-campus retreat to continue their discussions. The aforementioned changes in search committee processes began in these discussions and also involved faculty returning from the Multicultural Forums who formed the Diversity Action Committee.

As other colleges began to sponsor Multicultural Forums, the retreat for faculty women became an important event that created conversation and identified issues among women faculty. In October 2003, the College of Science held a retreat and in February 2004 the College of Agriculture held one. These meetings linked and engaged the women faculty who often were isolated in faculties that were heavily male. The three questions above were the focus of conversation and allowed the development of a format for the Gender Forum that included both men and women. In 2004, when the Multicultural Forums were phased in to all the rest of the University, there were more women faculty already present in most schools and colleges so that meetings of all the women faculty from a college were not as essential.

The Gender Forum: Final Format

Unlike the Multicultural Forums that took on a format early that was then adjusted as feedback and events in the outside world dictated, the Gender Forum took longer to emerge and has taken on several formats. This may be due partly to the very different situation with regard to the number of women faculty in the ten schools and colleges, which leads to different issues that may need to be addressed. It also has to do with the age and experience of the women faculty who may be involved. Women who have lived in academia through the 1970s bring a different history of experience than women more recently entering the academic workplace. Understanding and appreciating those differences is part of the agenda.

Forum Goals

All Purdue colleges can send faculty and staff men and women to the Gender Forum after they have participated in the Multicultural Forum. The goals of this two-day off-campus forum are twofold.

Collectively, the forum aims "to increase our competence in understanding the roles of gender and sexual orientation in how we prepare students for today's world." Individually, the forum aspires "for each of us to take personal responsibility for an environment of gender equity and balance in all aspects of our schools and in our lives." The forum is structured to provide "a safe situation where both genders can take some more steps toward honest dialogue and deeper understanding of one another's professional and life circumstances, as well as of the institutional helps and hindrances we can affect together."[6] There are specific goals in three areas:

- Awareness: To increase knowledge and understanding of the experiences that persons of a different gender have at Purdue
- Skills: To practice engaging others who are different so that you can comfortably do this back at the University
- The academic environment: To take actions that will make the campus environment more supportive and inclusive of everyone.

These goals parallel those of the Multicultural Forum but are in the area of gender and identity. The hope for the future is to create a culture where people can be fully who they are, women and men, gay and straight, and all the other diversities.

Forum Design

What is the process for this exploration? The forum begins with reminders of some of the Multicultural Forum ground rules and interpersonal skills. This training helped people engage and explore complex and sometimes unsettling issues in the Multicultural Forum. Then, the three person consulting staff—Janice Eddy, Bill Page, and Barbara Berry—asks the 30-40 participants to form groups based on how long they have been working at Purdue. The task of these groups is to talk about what the Purdue culture was like around gender and sexual orientation issues when they arrived at Purdue and whether anything has changed over time. These groups meet and then report to the whole. After all the reports, there is general reflection about what people noticed and patterns observed.

After a break, new groups are formed: two faculty groups, one male and one female; two staff groups, one male and one female. They are asked to discuss and report on two questions:

1. What gets in your way when you try to be colleagues across gender, sexual orientation, culture or class?
2. What do we need to know about each other—across gender, sexual orientation, culture, class?

These groups report after lunch in a series of same-sex and mixed-sex groupings interspersed with conversations in the group as a whole. What has happened is a day-long structured conversation about complex issues that people are often hesitant to voice or may be unaware of. In this setting, they engage in a level of conversation that is deeper than the usual talk that they are used to. People are surprised by what they learn and begin to understand. This enables them to return to campus with skills for conversations much deeper than the "politically correct." The staff report that there are some common themes, but that each forum is different depending on who comes.

Typical Gender Forum Themes

Faculty women: They don't feel really listened to or heard by male faculty colleagues. Time is wasted because the men take up a great deal of the airtime in groups and in conversations. It's difficult to get heard, so women spend a lot of time and energy figuring out how to say their idea and when to say it. They feel they spend too much of their time "taking care of others," constantly paying attention to what men are feeling and thinking so that they can figure out how to get their message across.

Faculty men: They didn't understand how much time women were spending accommodating men's wishes and trying to read men's behaviors. At one forum after the women listened to the men report what they understood the women to be saying, a woman faculty member got tears in her eyes because it was the first time in many, many years that she had felt really heard by her male colleagues.

Faculty women feel that men have lots of misconceptions and don't really know what their lives are like. This includes all kinds of women—single, married, with children. Many men give career advice without understanding the context of a woman's life.

Staff women say men they work with don't know them as people and they are not treated as a member of a team. Men expect them to respond to whatever is asked without knowing their work context and priorities.

Some women still feel that they get labeled negatively if they speak up for their own point of view too frequently or too vigorously.

Faculty and Staff Men: The majority of the men's comments are around their discomfort in forming peer relationships in the workplace with the other gender. On the one hand, the relationship can be misunderstood in terms of sexuality. On the other hand, they have no confidence in women's ability to take directness. So, they are careful and hedge what they say in relation to women. As a result, women often don't get accurate feedback about what the man is thinking.

The morning of day two is spent engaging the issue of sexual orientation and gender identity/expression. This exploration is facilitated by five skilled graduate and undergraduate students who are representatives of the Queer Student Union and the Ally Association and faculty and staff volunteers. They present information, involve the group in activities, and share personally from their experiences. Over the last few years, people coming to the Gender Forum have been increasingly eager to talk about and learn about issues of sexual orientation/values. They feel and express gratitude to the panel for their willingness to talk openly about their lives. This session is valued as one of the learning highlights of the Gender Forum.

The final afternoon begins by building an agenda from the previous day-and-a-half of issues and questions that the group still wishes to pursue and organizing to make that happen. At the end of the afternoon, small groups consider the impact of this experience on their future action and they make individual plans and commitments.[7]

The Numbers and Evaluating the Gender Forums

As of December 2008, 581 faculty and staff have attended a Gender Forum.

Since the Gender Forum developed more slowly and has had several different designs, a formal evaluation over time would be difficult. There is always, however, a final participant evaluation at the end of every forum and these data are available. The data reported here are taken from six recent Gender Forums from spring 2004 through spring 2007.

Overall Evaluation

One-hundred-and-seventy-five faculty, staff, and alumni attended these six recent forums. Evaluations were completed by 80.6% of those attending. The overall average evaluation of these forums on a seven-point scale where 1 is "awful" and 7 is "excellent" was 6.08 (ranging from 5.8 to 6.3). The evaluation of the content presented and experienced at the forum was 6.13 (ranging from 5.7 to 6.4). When asked if they would recommend the forum to others almost everyone said "Yes." No one said "No"; no one said "Don't know." Six people (4.5%) said "Maybe." The Gender Forum received very high marks from most of the people who have attended during the last three years.

Written Comments

In the section of the evaluation that asks for written comments about what people liked best and did not like and suggestions for improvement, some comments appear across the six forums. There are many positive comments about the openness of the interactions and discussions. People also comment on how much new information they learned from the panels. The discussion of sexual orientation is clearly a highpoint for many participants. Here are a few examples:

- "I was concerned about being preached to, but it was a true dialogue and discussion of real issues . . . very worthwhile." (Male faculty)

- "The way we went below the superficial; asked some hard questions" (Female staff)
- "The opportunity to let men see what women are like together and the opportunity to see what men are like in a group of men" (Female faculty)
- "Listening to the women faculty talk" (Male faculty)
- "Brought up a lot of great issues on how men assume or control certain situations. . . . This will help me play a bigger role in encouraging the women in my office to step up." (Male staff)

There was great diversity among the comments on what people didn't like and suggestions. There were comments about the day being too long, although in one forum, a number of people wanted an additional day added to the forum. Some people suggested revisions in the workshop format, that is, more of this, less of that. There were a few comments about providing more action planning time and activity. For the most part, the comments were individual and not easily summarized.

Participants attend the Gender Forum from all the schools and colleges, so what they take back tends to be more personal than organizational. The Multicultural Forums were cosponsored by colleges and people attended with others from their school or college, so there was more opportunity for ideas to develop within the unit and be taken back leading to change.

PART THREE

CHANGES IN THE DIVERSITY OF PURDUE FACULTY 1997-2007

BARBARA BENEDICT BUNKER

CHANGES IN THE DIVERSITY OF PURDUE FACULTY, 1997-2007

Since the Multicultural Forums started in the academic year 1997-1998 and the Purdue website[8] that tracks changes in faculty statistics posts those analyses starting in the same year, it seems reasonable to use that data to look for changes toward greater diversity in the faculty. This section focuses on the three colleges that have been involved in this initiative the longest, Engineering, Science, and Agriculture. I think it is also fair to say these three colleges had a distance to go, especially with regard to the numbers of women faculty as compared with other colleges. Data for other colleges that began participating in the forums later has been included in the description of their participation and is also available on the Purdue website.

The numbers in Tables 1-3 (see Appendix A) speak for themselves. It is of course important to acknowledge that several factors have encouraged the changes reflected in the numbers. The Multicultural and Gender Forums were important at the college level. The decision of the administration to hire 300 new faculty members, 50% of whom would be women or minorities, during this period was also a major factor.

College of Engineering

Women

When the first forum was held in the College of Engineering in January 1998, several women respondents commented that there were only three full professors (role models) in engineering of the 127 tenured or tenure-track professors in engineering. Of the total engineering faculty of 267 only 17 (7.1%) were women. There were no female department heads or deans.

There has been a gradual but dramatic change in this picture over the ten-year period ending with the 2006-2007 academic year. Women are now 12.4% of engineering faculty (38 women with tenure or tenure-track lines of 307 faculty). In the ten-year period, the number of tenure-track women faculty has almost doubled. At the assistant professor level, women are now 31.7% of the incumbents, up from 11.6% in 1997-1998. This means that there is a substantial pipeline of future associate and full professors if the climate for their advancement is supportive.

Since 2002-2003, women have become much more visible in leadership roles. Two women have held the position of dean after national searches and other women faculty are currently associate and assistant deans. Woman head two of the ten departments.

Of course, many forces affect these numbers, but clearly there are important changes reported here that are greater than increases in the hiring of women in the faculty as a whole at Purdue in this period (an increase of 4%).

Minorities

Minority hiring in engineering follows a similar but less dramatic pattern. The percent of the tenure-track faculty that are minority increased over the ten-year period from 22.1% to 31.3%. However, a large proportion of minority faculty is Asian American or Hawaiian or Pacific Islander. The numbers for African Americans, Hispanics, and American Indians increased but are still small. Persons in these categories who are internationals rather than citizens of the United States went from 3% to 7.8% of tenure-track faculty. When we look only at tenure-track faculty by rank, all ranks increased their percentage within rank over the ten-year period. Full professors went from 21.5% to 29.7% minority (+8.2%); associate professors from 17.5% to 22.8% (+5.3); assistant professors from 34.9% to 46.0% (+11.1). Internationals did not comprise much of the increase in either professor or associate professor ranks, but there was a larger increase of internationals at the assistant professor rank (from 11.6% to 31.7%).

Colleges of Agriculture and Science

The College of Agriculture and the College of Science began participating regularly in the Muticultural Forums in spring 2002. This occurred shortly after President Jischke came to Purdue with a strong emphasis on diversity in his strategic plan for the University.

College of Agriculture: Women

In the College of Agriculture in 1997-1998, 10.2% of tenured and tenure-track faculty were women (28 of 275). This increased to 16.4% (49 of 299) in 2006-2007. In the ten-year period, the overall headcount of tenured and tenure-track faculty in agriculture increased by 24 positions. Interestingly, in agriculture there has been more of an increase in full professors and associate professors over the ten-year period than in assistant professors.

College of Agriculture: Minorities

Minority hiring in agriculture has increased for the total faculty from 6.2% (17 of 275) to 12.7% (38 of 299), with gains in all categories, but the biggest gains for Asian Americans and Hawaiian or Pacific Islanders. The percentage of minorities who are international did not increase greatly over ten years (from 2.2% to 3.3%).

College of Science: Women

In the College of Science, women were 10.0% of tenured and tenure-track faculty in 1997-98. In 2006-2007, women were 15.8% (+5.8%). In Science, there were increases in all ranks of women faculty over the ten years. Associate professors increased 4.3%, full professors increased 3.9%, and assistant professors increased 2.5%. In rank, women increased from being 3.8% of full professors in 1997-1998 to 7.7% in 2006-2007. Associate professors increased from 17.2% to 21.6% of their rank and assistant professors from 25.9% to 28.4%. In this same period, the percentage of professors decreased while the numbers of assistant professors increased. In real numbers, women professors almost doubled (from 7 to 13) while assistant professors tripled (from 7 to 21).

The Chemistry Department has a particularly high percentage of women (22%) as compared with other departments across the United States.[9] This is an increase from 13% in 1997. In leadership, a woman is an associate dean and there are two female heads of departments as well as one distinguished professor.

College of Science: Minorities

Minority faculty in the College of Science comprised 15.7% of faculty in 1997-1998. This rose to 28.3% in 2006-2007, an increase of 12.6%. Much of this increase is accounted for by increases in the number of Asian and Hawaiian or Pacific Islander faculty, which more than doubled during this period. The numbers for African Americans and Hispanics increased slightly. Internationals were 3.2% of faculty in 1997-1998 and increased to 7.6% in 2006-2007. Minority full professors increased 6% during this period (from 14.2% to 20.2%), minority associate professors increased 21.5% (from 13.8% to 35.3%); and minority assistant professors increased 11.3% (from 33.3% to 44.6%).

These data indicate what can happen when deans and college leadership make increasing faculty diversity a serious priority for their colleges. These initiatives became even more effective under the leadership of President Jischke and Provost Mason, who both emphasized and funded new faculty hiring with clear priorities about diversity.

PART FOUR

THE PROVOST PLANS FOR
THE WHOLE
ACADEMIC
ORGANIZATION

BARBARA BENEDICT BUNKER

The Provost Plans for the Whole Academic Organization

As the forums became established campus wide, Provost Mason began a discussion with Janice Eddy, her consultant on matters of diversity, about diversity issues in the University at large. Over a period of several years, they developed a strong working relationship. Janice Eddy thinks about organizations as systems, which means that to change the culture you need to encourage change at all levels of the system—individual, group, and as a whole. As she learned in more depth about the culture of Purdue through dialogue with a widely diverse group of people and as the Multicultural Forums became more and more established, she began to talk with the provost about some kind of university-wide group that would come together to think about the academic side of the University. The Diversity Leadership Group grew out of the provost's strong interest in moving the Purdue culture forward. The provost and her consultant worked collaboratively, taking on different leadership responsibilities at different stages of the group's development, as we shall see in the next section.

The Diversity Leadership Group (DLG)

The Diversity Leadership Group, as an advisory group to the provost, came together for the first time in fall 2004. Membership was invited by the provost from all the colleges and relevant areas throughout the University. People felt personally "tapped by the provost" but also pleased that she told them they were free to buy in or buy out. The group is very diverse with regard to race, ethnicity, and gender. It includes faculty and staff from all the colleges.

IN THEIR OWN WORDS: MARY SADOWSKI
ASSOCIATE DEAN OF THE COLLEGE OF TECHNOLOGY AND MEMBER OF THE DIVERSITY LEADERSHIP GROUP

About the Diversity Leadership Group (DLG)
The first couple of meetings were awkward and quiet. But everyone in the group felt tapped by the provost personally. She told us we could buy in or buy out. Sally came and spent her time in day long retreats. She gave her time and her energy, so how could we not?

We have developed a relationship and we feel we know each other. There is very little we are uncomfortable saying. Everyone contributes: We are open and honest but we think before we talk. The *Mosaic* is a beautifully written document, and I am hoping it is going to be our road map.

Establishing an Open and Safe Environment

The provost, Sally Mason, asked Janice Eddy to orchestrate the early sessions so that she could participate more fully. Initially, the agenda of the group was not very clear except that they were the provost's advisory group on matters of diversity. Interviews with members described the early meetings as not very comfortable. People did not know each other nor did they trust each other. A major agenda during their first year was to be able to develop relationships within the group that would allow people to speak honestly with each other. The provost modeled this behavior by using the group as a sounding board from time to time about diversity issues confronting her in her role as provost. She also signaled the importance of the group by giving it a significant amount of her time (two- or three-hour meetings once a month and a two-day retreat). People commented about how refreshing it was to get to know her and interact with her as a person.

Managing the Group Dynamics

Group members also commented on Janice Eddy's skill in facilitating the sometimes difficult first phase of group development.

Her skill in the dynamics of getting people to talk, open up, accept others' feelings, and suspend evaluation were seen as essential during the first six months. By the end of the first year, most people said that the DLG had really become a team exploring the campus climate of diversity and working on a future plan for diversity for the colleges. From the early meetings, where one member said she saw the need to "fiercely protect what you have got and that isn't enough," the group became a safe, even friendly environment where people could speak freely and expect to be listened to with respect and understanding.

The DLG Meets the Diversity Directors

The two-day off-campus retreat in March 2006 was cited as a turning point in the life of the group. All the diversity directors from the colleges were invited to join the DLG for part of their retreat and talk about their views of the past, present, and future of diversity at Purdue. These were administrators who had worked at the grass roots level and were most knowledgeable about the Purdue culture. Their perspectives and their experiences at Purdue and in the community had strong impact on the DLG.

The *Mosaic:* A Diversity Master Plan for Purdue

As the DLG developed a strong substantive agenda and a capacity to deal openly with differences within the group, Janice Eddy's role shifted. She became more of a gentle gadfly in suggesting questions or issues that were being ignored and needed attention. One respondent noted that because Eddy isn't part of Purdue or an engineer, "She can do things that a technical person can't. She does not compete with the engineers so they feel OK. We have to have someone who will continue to be a sounding board and asking those questions that only Janice can ask with her little laugh."

In this phase, the Provost chaired the meetings and led the work on what became the vision and action plan for diversity at Purdue. The document the DLG produced is entitled *Toward a Mosaic for Educational Equity,* which is usually simply referred to as "the *Mosaic.*" The document articulates a vision of diversity at Purdue and describes seven key strategies: Recruitment, Professional Development and Advancement, Retention, Pedagogy, Research and Scholarship, the Intellectual Environment, and Climate. Each key strategy includes proposed actions and metrics for measuring achievements. The document concludes with 12 Key Priorities for the immediate future and a funding estimate to realize these priorities. The work of the group culminated in a campus-wide celebration in February 2007 with the roll out of the *Mosaic* document.[10]

IN THEIR OWN WORDS: ELI ASEM
PROFESSOR, SCHOOL OF VETERINARY MEDICINE

About the Diversity Leadership Group (DLG):
It took several meetings to learn about each other. The process was not manipulated. Things flowed naturally. The outcome was what the group wanted and not what the provost desired.

The *Mosaic* is an active document; we will all use it. It will serve as the foundation for the Purdue culture as far as diversity is concerned. It speaks to and about everybody. Everyone is included; no one is left out. That's why it will succeed. It will take time for different units to implement it.

Implementing the *Mosaic*

The next phase is to follow their map of the future by moving forward on the 12 Key Priorities. In spring 2007, the DLG became a permanent advisory group reporting to the provost. They created a process for rotating off some members each year and bringing on new members. Everyone who wanted to stay on was able to do so and they then drew lots for length of term to create the rotational system.

Diversity across the Campus and in the Larger Community

In 1997-1998, only three or four colleges had diversity directors, and they were largely concerned with the programmatic work of recruiting and retaining women and minorities. As deans attended the forums, they came to see the value to the college of such a role. Over time this role has emerged as an important one at the policy level within the colleges. As of this writing, all the colleges now have directors of diversity, many of whom report directly to the dean and sit on committees that decide policy. Within the last few years, a regular monthly meeting of diversity directors across the University has been held. As a group, they are now sharing information and learning from each other, developing priorities for action, and having more influence collectively. We see here another integrating structure like the Diversity Leadership Group that is knitting together efforts once made in isolation.

The Forum Coordinators Network

A critical piece of infrastructure that makes the forums possible is the group of faculty, the associate deans, diversity directors, and staff assistants in each school or college who register people for the forums and recruit alumni and student participants. Not only are they key to making these events happen, but they are important sources of information about how the events are going and what needs to be improved. At the beginning of each semester, this group meets with Janice Eddy to make plans and share learnings and suggestions. They both support the forums and each other in making them successful.

Administrative Initiatives

There are other structures within the administrative structure of Purdue University that are also moving in this direction. Alysa Rollick, Vice President of Ethics and Compliance, formerly Vice President of Human Relations, and her staff developed training programs for staff and conducts the all-campus climate survey on diversity every five years, which is an important measure of campus culture. Carolyn Johnson, Director of the Diversity Resource Office, and Interim Chief Diversity Officer, convenes the Purdue University Roundtable that meets five times a year and brings together people from both the academic and the administrative sides of the University who are involved in diversity education to share information, work on projects, and coordinate efforts. Several people from the administrative side of the University expressed concern about the lack of communication and coordination between what is happening in the colleges with faculty and staff and what is happening in student services with students' co-curricular activities both on campus and as they do community service.

PART FIVE

CHANGING UNIVERSITIES AS SYSTEMS

BARBARA BENEDICT BUNKER

CHANGING UNIVERSITIES AS SYSTEMS

In this section, we will take a look at universities as targets of change and also describe the theory of intervention and the action strategies of Janice Eddy, the consultant to this diversity initiative.

Diversity initiatives usually involve experiential learning at the individual level so that the members of the organization will have more knowledge and personal awareness of both their own cultural or ethnic group and of others. As one of the staff of the Multicultural Forum said: "In order to build authentic relationships, you have to know yourself. This means for many stepping out of your comfort zone." People are only willing to do that if they feel safe, which is why the forums are structured to be supportive rather than confrontational. For that reason, new issues of diversity are only added to the forum when the culture feels ready to engage them. For example, a unit on the Middle East was introduced after the 9/11 attack. Sexual orientation was introduced in the Gender Forum when President Jischke acknowledged that it should be included in discussions of diversity at the university level and when the forum coordinators felt it was an issue that was timely and needed to be included. The forum staff have been talking about how and when to introduce religion for some time. Diversity issues that involve class, mixed-race identity, and issues of assimilation are all waiting in the wings.

At another level of diversity, organizational systems have policies and procedures, formal and informal ways of doing things that may send subtle and not so subtle messages to members of underrepresented groups about their welcome and treatment in the organization.

IN THEIR OWN WORDS: JEFF WRIGHT
DEAN OF ENGINEERING, UNIVERSITY OF CALIFORNIA AT MERCED

That first workshop was very influential. My first discussion after the Forum was with Carolyn Percifield about how our programs could benefit from faculty going to the forums. At the next dean's meeting, we raised the question of how to keep the forums going. With Dick's support and encouragement (and funding!) we had good success over the next few years involving faculty in this extremely valuable experience.

Klod Kokini, one of the echanical engineering faculty who participated in the workshops early on, and who was subsequently appointed to the dean's staff as Assistant Dean (Jeff Wright became Associate Dean), enthusiastically joined this effort. With Klod and a few other key faculty, the Schools' Diversity Action Committee (DAC) emerged to discuss how we could more proactively internalize the experience from the forums into the operations of the schools. Our goal was to get thorough consideration of diversity, representation, and inclusiveness into every major policy discussion within the schools, from curriculum development and design, to faculty recruiting and hiring. This itself was no small task, but as we had more and more faculty who had participated in the forums, it became easier. Change was starting to happen not from the top down—at least not perceptibly—but from the bottom up. We were succeeding: what the faculty "own" in a research university will be sustained.

I am proud of what we accomplished. Though I am no longer at Purdue, I understand that the DAC concept has continued to spread within Engineering and across campus, with leadership in the other major schools. I wish we could take credit for the fact that following these early efforts, the School of Engineering has now had two women deans, several faculty of color in key leadership positions, and now its first woman president. Whatever the reason, Purdue maintains its stature as a premier engineering school, and is certainly playing a major role in expanding the much needed diversity in the profession. The DAC certainly didn't hurt.

Janice Eddy was hired initially by the College of Engineering to work with faculty and staff at the individual (training) level, because the faculty and staff have the greatest impact on the culture of the institution, especially as it involves students. If faculty and staff develop more understanding and skills to enable them to cross cultural boundaries, they have the capacity to change their own culture. Dean Schwartz's intuitive sense that only a faculty-driven initiative could create real change fits this way of thinking.

The Crucial Role of Alumni and Students

In planning the forums, the first question Janice Eddy considered was "Who will faculty and staff really listen to? Who will they consider credible?" Outsiders might be interesting and able to deliver new information, but they do not have the emotional impact of insiders. Eddy believes that experiential learning involves creating relationships in which people get new information and are touched by that information. Hearing the experiences and stories of people who are or have been their students or colleagues makes the information more salient and personal at the same time. This means they might take it seriously and try something new themselves back in their college or classroom. For these reasons, each forum is about 10% alums or students from underrepresented groups.

An External Consultant with an Inside Team

Eddy does not see her work as simply running training events. She spends time developing relationships within the organization as part of her work with the system. In part, she needs to do this in order to understand the institution and create an experience that will fit the members of that organization. Because her work is about diversity, she reaches out to get to know minorities and women because she wants to understand their experience at Purdue. She also networks because she needs opinion leaders in the University to understand what the Multicultural Forums are about and support them. Finally, the conversations that develop in personal relationships help her to think about what should happen next in her work in the University. Some of this is an exchange of tangible ideas and some of it builds an intuitive base that is the source of her ideas. So, for example, building relationships with diversity directors in the colleges was key to her understanding the diversity work that had already been done and the culture of the University from their perspective. Likewise, after 9/11, Kamyar Haghighi, Head of Engineering Education and Professor of Agriculture and Biological Engineering, Rabi Mohtar, Professor in Agricultural and Biological Engineering, and Atossa Rahmanifar, Epidemiologist for the State of Indiana, helped her to develop a unit on the Middle East. As she met people through the forums or had people brought to her attention, she reached out to build a relationship that might inform her work. Some of these people have become an informal network where she can try out new ideas or ask about issues she does not have the background to understand. This cadre of internal supporters and truth-tellers are often critical to the success of an external consultant. No matter how talented an external consultant is, they do not live and breathe the organization as true members of the system.

Sustaining Culture Change

Eddy is working to effect change in the system, not just give people a good personal experience. She is always asking herself, "How can this work be sustained?" She looked for ways to move the forums into all the colleges so that there would be a wider impact. She looked for faculty and staff who could be connected so that they would sustain the work. She encouraged deans to support faculty-driven initiatives such as the Diversity Action Committees that formed in many colleges after faculty returned from participating in the Multicultural Forum experiences. In the same way, she has encouraged colleges to jointly sponsor the forums, partly because it allows faculties to interact and spreads good ideas from one college to another. She herself has planted ideas like seeds in places where she thought they might grow.

Influence and Power in Universities

Unlike business organizations where executives have the power to make and enforce decisions, universities are "professional bureaucracies" (Mintzberg, 1979).[11] These are organizations in which power is less centralized. The administration has a certain power but the faculty, for example, control the curriculum and have a strong hand in recruiting new faculty and in their promotion and tenure. Thus, if the administration wants to create a more favorable, accepting culture within the University for women and minorities, they can let that be known in strategic plans, mission statements, and the allocation of resources and personal leadership, but they depend on the faculty and staff to implement those plans, to make them happen. They can bring to bear informal pressure, but they don't have the power to fire, demote, or, for that matter, promote people without faculty participation in the decision making. Unlike business, the people at the bottom of the hierarchy are all PhDs with a great deal of structural autonomy to do their research and teach. The goal here is for these two parts of the University to collaborate to move forward. Power is shared, not centralized.

Resisting the Impulse to Create Structures

Eddy has interesting ideas about structure. She believes that structure comes later, after you have people acting on good ideas and engaging each other. If you start by appointing a committee or creating a role you may interfere with the natural development that needs to occur. Too often good energy dissipates in the face of a too early created structure. What makes more sense, she believes, is to wait and see what structures develop naturally and help them along rather than to impose a structure too soon. An example is the university-wide Diversity Leadership Group. As a consultant to the provost since 2003, this could have been proposed much earlier, but Eddy's intuition was that the forums needed to be university wide and there needed to be a critical mass of people who had had the forum experience before a university-wide structure would be sustainable. So she waited several years until some faculty began to talk about the need for university-wide strategic planning for diversity to suggest to the provost that she might form such a group. Initially, this group was ad hoc. Recently the structure has been made official.

Another example is the informal Diversity Action Committee that developed spontaneously in Engineering. It only became an official structure after a number of years of acting informally (but with the encouragement of the dean). There are also several examples of deans of colleges creating a structural opportunity for a faculty member who is innovating around diversity in the classroom to share what they are doing with other faculty. At the university level, Dorothy Reed's position as Assistant Provost was created in part as a structure to support the implementation of the *Mosiac*. The rule of thumb is to use structure to support promising initiatives rather than to expect a structure to create them.

Working with individuals in systems requires understanding how organizations work and how they get changed as well as relationship skills to connect across boundaries in the service of creating a community that supports people while it embraces their differences.

INTO THE FUTURE

Ten years has seen marked changes at Purdue, but as the recent campus survey of the diversity climate reveals,[12] there are still areas where there is much to do. The Multicultural and Gender Forums continue to inform and touch faculty and staff, the shapers of campus culture. This narrative documents a sustained ten-year process and some of the outcomes that we know about. Provost Sally Mason, whose strong leadership and personal and financial support was critical to this initiative, left Purdue in August 2007 to become the president of the University of Iowa. The new provost and president will write the next chapter, but in the context of trends in higher education that reflect a much more urgent awareness of the importance of diversity in the education of students. There is a national conversation about different ways to teach science, technology, and engineering that can engage the different learning styles of the increasingly diverse next generation. Radical proposals are being sought and seriously contemplated. Students are demanding instruction in the world's languages. More and more colleges and universities are sending students abroad to study as part of their undergraduate experience.

Purdue University was light years ahead of other universities when this diversity initiative, which directly involves faculty and staff, started. What will come next at Purdue?

POSTSCRIPT

This kind of research is deeply involving because as the researcher, you are trying to understand as fully as you can the point of view and experience of each person you talk with. Then it is your job to take all the interviews and materials you have studied and make sense of it around the original research goal of documenting what has happened. It is not possible to have been engaged with faculty, staff, and administration at Purdue for more that 60 hours of interviews without coming to some personal thoughts and reactions. As a person who studies and consults to organizations as well as being a professor of psychology, what has happened at Purdue seems to me quite remarkable. I have been intensely involved in this research project for more than a year, and as I prepare to let this document see the light of day and be read by others there are a few ideas about the way forward that I would like to underline, although they come from the people I talked with.

At the college level, there has been important support from the dean's office for both forums and for initiatives from the faculty and staff around diversity issues. This report documents the real institutional gains that changes in policies and procedures have brought within most of the colleges. Minorities and women report that some very important changes have occurred that are improving the sense of welcoming community. However, I did not get any sense that "we have arrived where we want to be." There is still more to do, new initiatives to be created, before what has begun will be fully realized. There is widespread agreement among the people I talked with, including consultants, faculty, administration and in the evaluation data that the follow-up process after the forums needs to take more advantage of the motivation and learning that occurs there. For these initiatives to become sustainable, they have to become embedded in the culture, to become new traditions, policies, and ways of doing things here. Some colleges are doing more than others, but this is an area with real possibilities for development.

There are currently various attempts to bring together people across the campus who are moving this new sense of community forward. As these people work together, a clearer idea of how to involve the whole campus will hopefully emerge. One undeveloped aspect of the broader campus integration is finding the best way for faculty on campus whose research area involves multicultural, diversity, or gender studies (to name only the most obvious areas) to make a real contribution to the development of this new culture at Purdue.

It is clear that the diversity initiative would not have had the impact it has had across the University without the strong leadership of the former president and provost. In Provost Mason's hands-on leadership she gave time and verbal support and made decisions that made very clear to everyone that this was a personal as well as a university priority. Hopefully, the new leadership of Purdue will support the implementation of the *Mosiac* and other new initiatives as effectively.

PART SIX

PERSPECTIVES:
THE
OUTSIDE CONSULTANT
REFLECTS AND
LOOKS AHEAD

JANICE EDDY

.

Perspectives: The Outside Consultant Reflects and Looks Ahead

In this section, I consider my own journey during the ten years I have worked with Purdue University. It begins with my understanding of my general consulting role and then describes both the learning and the theory development that I and the Multicultural Forum staff have achieved as we tailored the forums to the Purdue culture.

Consulting Rules of Thumb and Lessons Learned[13]

Lesson 1. Start small, think big.

It was my belief from the outset that the forums could go beyond individual learning and be a catalyst for institutional culture change by energizing dialogue and action across the University. Both of those agendas were always in the forefront of my thinking.

Lesson 2. Enter a new system as an anthropologist, not with a grand plan, model, or template.

Pre-models, templates, and grand plans of failed culture-change efforts litter the corridors of institutions. They are built on the notion that in the consultant resides the knowledge of what *should* be happening and how. Anthropologists instead see what is there

My experience has shown me that I have wider and more sustained success in new initiatives if I observe, listen a lot, and let the people I get to know teach me. The education I have gained through the people of Purdue continues to guide my actions and the advice I give.

Lesson 3. Be patient, "labor in the vineyards," earn trust.

My unofficial consulting role began a number of years before Provost Mason officially hired me in that capacity. The Colleges of Engineering, Science, and Agriculture did not have budgets for an external consultant.

I believe that in any new project it is important to "labor in the vineyards" initially, so I spent many hours before and after forums building relationships and educating myself about the colleges and schools. This provided me with a solid foundation for moving initiatives across the University.

Lesson 4. Build credibility and trust with marginalized people.

It was important to me from the outset, especially as a white woman, to gain credibility and build trust with staff and faculty who have been marginalized in the University and in society generally. In Purdue's case this meant largely black members of our community, as initially there were few other domestic minorities who were Latino, Native American, or Asian American.

Marian Blalock introduced me to senior black leaders, while Thelma Snuggs introduced me to the Black Caucus and invited me to teach a session of one of her undergraduate classes. I met other black faculty and staff members in the forums, as well as a few Latinos, Native Americans, and Asian Americans. I made it a point to visit these new colleagues and the predominantly black diversity directors in each college or school whenever I was on campus, continuing to deepen our relationships and learn as much as I could from them.

Being in the trenches and having endured for many years, they were able to enlighten me about currents in the emotional underground around issues of race; I then brought that information to the provost for her consideration and action. They also contributed to my personal learning as a white woman working on race, sometimes through my mistakes and their graciousness in correcting me.

Lesson 5. Cross-pollinate ideas; engage in honey bee consulting.[14]

Working with Provost Mason gave me access to many parts of the academic system, allowing me to find out what was already in progress concerning diversity goals and efforts across Purdue—the hopes, successes, failures, stuck places, gaps, and learnings. I was enabled to identify and get to know many of the significant people involved.

I learned that there were few ways for the colleges and schools to learn from one anothers' experience. There was as yet no designated person in the provost's office to gather and disseminate this information. As I moved among them and absorbed information, I took on the role of connector, encourager, and cross-pollinator of ideas across the ten colleges and schools.

Lesson 6: Suggest and nourish new supporting infrastructure when needed and timely.

One of my roles with Provost Mason was to suggest new infrastructure and positions for the support and institutionalization of changes in diversity culture. Our discussions led to the creation of:

- The provost's Diversity Leadership Group (DLG)
- The Multicultural-Minority Program Directors (MMPD): the regular meeting of diversity directors and others to provide support, information sharing, and development
- The assistant provost for diversity, a position held by Dorothy Reed

Lesson 7. The importance of having an inside consulting partner cannot be overestimated.

As an outsider, it is not always possible at the outset to select a consulting partner. His or her helpfulness resides less in a designated role than in a passion for the topic, persistence, broad perspectives, wide connections, a willingness to learn, and an ability to be in a mutually supportive and honest relationship.

As an external consultant, my effectiveness is a direct result of a partnership with an internal person who shares my passion, understands the political landscape of the system, and can talk with me on a daily basis as needed. The foundation for this partnership consists of mutual empowerment and an openness to learning.

My partner turned out to be Barbara Clark, Director of Diversity for the College of Science. We had developed a good working relationship as I became involved with the College. When Provost Mason asked me to consult with her, she also asked for one quarter of Clark's time to manage the forums and other diversity matters.

There is a lesson here, too. When I asked Barbara what she had learned over the past years, she said, and I paraphrase:

> Working with you, I have learned to be a consultant rather than a teacher. For example, formerly, if a local public school asked me to help them with a student race issue, I would have prepared a decent talk, given it, and afterwards felt little satisfaction. I think the same reaction would be true for my audience, though they didn't expect more. Little would change in the school system itself.
>
> Now I ask the school to gather a few interested teachers and maybe some students for a small meeting where we can discuss all the relevant history, context, significant players, and aspects of their problem. Then, together we plan an event to which I bring a partner—in this case a black woman—so there are not just white people up front facilitating an event about race. Afterwards, I get feedback about the event and the changes it has set into motion. I feel I've been more helpful and have made some new relationships. I find this approach more organic and adaptable, and as a result I have become more flexible, more humanized.

Barbara's clear thinking, caring, constant support, and honest feedback, especially when I have overlooked something or someone or become inflexible on some issue or made mistakes, empowered me to take more risks, be more innovative, trust myself, and be more human.

Lesson 8. Gradually build an ad hoc internal support system for yourself.

Look for people who have a passion for the issues, understand the politics, make good sounding boards, give you feedback, and can help you avoid land mines. It is important that these people be of different races, nationalities, genders, sexual orientations, and ages. They need to come from different levels in the university hierarchy and include students. It is not important that they meet as a group.

Lesson 9. Use external consultants and friends to consult with you.

I called on other consultants in the field of diversity training to provide perspective when I felt stuck. Because they had no stake in the client system and knew both my strengths and flat sides, they were able to open up new ways of thinking for me. I also gave updates on the Purdue project at three yearly meetings of the Portsmouth Consulting Group, in which I have membership. They gave me feedback from an organization development and change point of view.

PERSONAL LEARNINGS

As an Organizational Development consultant, I believe that we in our field are both expert and continually learning. What follow are some important learnings for me personally over the last ten years.

Lesson 1. Changing my consulting role in a culture new to me.

Having been trained as a process consultant, it was a steep learning curve for me to comfortably emphasize my expertise in conjunction with my seed-planting role. I think this speaks to the high value placed on intellectual power and logic in academia, compared to action power and meeting the bottom line in the corporate world.

One of my preferred learning styles is intuition. It was difficult to keep trusting this in a culture that places a high value on hard data. In this new culture where I was marginal, my most creative ideas arrived in bursts or awakenings or at the last minute, rather than through reasoned analysis; for example, building the forums around the minority alumni, and including the diversity directors to provide history and current feedback at the first DLG offsite on diversity strategic planning, which eventually led to *Mosaic*.

Lesson 2. Growing deeper respect for engineering and science research.

My degree work was in Liberal Arts, because I never felt at home in the sciences or math, never mind engineering. My Purdue experiences have given me a new respect for and interest in all of these areas. I found commonality in the shared love for clarity, innovation, and creativity. I discovered deep admiration for the intellectual openness and willingness to be touched emotionally in my new research-oriented colleagues.

Lesson 3. Letting go of stereotypes and building on integrity.

Admittedly, being an easterner and from a small Ohio liberal arts college with graduate studies in Applied Behavioral Science and Diversity, I entered Purdue with some uncomfortable stereotypes about traditional Midwestern Big Ten Universities and my ability to fit in enough to help make some changes. It took me some time to let go of these, to clearly see the people I have come to know as fellow colleagues and truth seekers in diversity, and to trust the promise of the future for Purdue.

I believe that the people of Purdue combine deep integrity and midwestern kindness, and with innovative leaders increasing the number of people whose cultures have been marginal, Purdue is already building the inclusive community we are working toward. It is my great privilege to be part of this extraordinary journey.

LESSONS LEARNED: THE CONSULTANTS AS CHANGE AGENTS

To capture these lessons, I combed through my past ten years, then interviewed the team of forum consultants and my internal partner, Barbara Clark. Many, many Purdue people have been our teachers. We have learned as much or more than we have taught. As one of the consultants said, "It has been humbling. Purdue people have had a major effect on us professionally and we have each grown personally as well. For this, we are deeply grateful. Coming out of many years consulting in the corporate world, we had no inkling how much we would be changed by being part of a culture-change effort in an organization dedicated not to the bottom line, but to human growth."

What follows in this section are some of the key lessons that popped up suddenly, crept up on us over time, or wore down our own resistances to new learning that we unknowingly carried into Purdue. It is our hope that they may be useful to Purdue people who champion inclusion and also serve as guidelines for change agents in other universities and colleges.

As the forums' consulting team for more than sixty forums, we can identify four learning stages we have gone through in our own development at Purdue: Excitement and Trepidation, Proving our Expertise, Resistance and Struggle, Humility and Respect. One problem with stage theory framework is that it looks linear on paper when in reality it is anything but. It also appears to assume a final stage when there is in fact no final stage to such a dynamic process. But it can identify turning points along the journey.

With each successive stage the forum designs improved. As we go forward, we will repeatedly revisit them as new information, people, and events challenge our assumptions and our thinking about these issues.

Stage I: Excitement and Trepidation

Lesson 1. Invite minority participants to be partners in creating the learning process.

We found it was critical to include in the education and recommendations for action the experience of people from minority cultures for whom the University wants to create a more welcoming, inclusive community.

At the outset there were just three of us, Richard Orange, Bill Page, and I. Richard, a dear colleague to all of us, passed away suddenly after we facilitated just two forums; Barbara Berry took his place. Rosaura Aida Cepeda, Ann Kusumoto, and Atossa Rahmanifar came on board during Provost Mason's watch.

We were excited about working in academia after so many years in the corporate world. Though experienced, we were anxious about our lack of academic credentials—we are neither PhDs nor engineers. I worried about whether the Engineering faculty and staff would listen to us and participate seriously.

Doing errands one day, I found myself having the following conversation with myself: "Who do academics listen to? If not us, then who?" An answer followed quickly: "Students! Academics listen to and care about their students." My inner conversation continued: "If we include students of color to talk about their Purdue experiences and make recommendations for change, wouldn't this setting be too intimidating? Probably. But what about alumni of color? Aha.....that would work!"

Stage II: Proving our Expertise

Lesson 2. Find innovative ways to involve research scientists in their own self-exploration.

We knew we had a successful nationwide track record in helping businesses, secondary schools, government agencies and not-for-profit organizations address their diversity issues. The task would be to apply our knowledge, experience, and approach in a totally different culture. We proceeded much as we had in these other worlds, emphasizing human relations theory and practice with a focus on feelings as the building blocks for exploration and dialogue about diversity issues, specifically race, culture, gender, and sexual orientation.

Research academics seek new truths. They expect hard data and accurate statistics and are most at home with dialogue in the cognitive arena, not the feelings and subconscious arenas. We wrestled with how to invite people in this majority group to learn in a different, less familiar style.

The issue was how to provide the winning balance of conceptual and emotional input to touch them while also stimulating their curiosity about the experiences of minority people and about their own race/culture and its impact on others.

Lesson 3. The forum needs to acknowledge the expertise of academic people who have experience or scholarship in diversity issues and invite them to share their learning during the session.

We struggled with how best to include the knowledge of academics without slipping into the expert model of education. As one of the consultants said: "Our pedagogy is quite different than the pedagogy we have walked into. Our data comes from cumulative experience.…We've heard thousands of stories over the years. The foundation of our work is anecdotal. Our base is 'please tell me your experience and I will work to understand it.' The University base is often 'I have knowledge to impart to you; then I will ask you to share your reactions or experience.'"

Lesson 4. University personnel expect that international people must transition into a new culture at Purdue, but may not know this is also true for many minority people.

Significant numbers of Purdue people did not see domestic minorities as having a distinct culture. They did not realize that these people experience being marginalized in the majority culture of Purdue.

This news throws some majority culture people into individual versions of shock, disbelief, denial, awakening, sadness, guilt, distancing, or resentment. It is also a shock to most of the minority alumni that the majority is not aware of this. The consultants constantly work to develop even better ways to lead people through this new information and their reactions without shutting them down.

Lesson 5. When people seem overly cautious or even silent where issues of race, gender, and LGBTQ issues are being explored in more depth than usual, find out what is preventing conversation.

In the early Gender Forums we discovered that some women Engineering faculty were silencing themselves so as not to express past pain publicly or incur future career limitations. The antidote was to stop the forums temporarily while bringing the women together for support, healing, and action.

At the Multicultural Forums, some white men and women are silent initially because they resent being sent or they feel targeted. Some of this silence is due to discomfort with the unfamiliar personal dialogue; some is because people are wary of being labeled a bigot. Many of the women staff had never been in a learning environment of this type, nor with faculty present.

Given the unusual mix of participants, we continually redesign the first day of the forum to provide a welcoming, safe, open, and engaging multicultural environment. We have also experimented with different time frames to honor the juggling of classes or family that everyone goes through in order to attend.

Stage III: Resistance and Struggle

Lesson 6. Resistance and struggle are part of this territory for participants and for the consultants. Enduring and coming through the rough spots hinges on the strength of relationships, both professional and personal, among people championing inclusion.

In the early forums the team struggled to hang in when our learning curve was so steep and our experience and results not satisfying. Criticism mounted about meeting offsite and overnight, then meeting nearer campus but starting Sunday afternoons and two evenings, while we felt we needed three days to accomplish the forum goals.

As negative feedback accumulated alongside positive remarks, we struggled with our own resistance to change and our own contradictions. That is, we believed that the important learning resides in the participants while simultaneously believing that we were the experts in educational content and process.

We continually struggled to lessen some white participants' resentment about the forum sections on White Culture and Racism. That struggle continues. We also struggle to not fall in the trap of thinking and talking as if the race issue is about Black and White, dropping out Native Americans, Latinos, Asians, Asian Americans and mixed-race people.

The consultants still struggle to do a better job of including the experiences of international faculty and staff. This bumps up against our primary charge, which is to help build an inclusive community with an emphasis on increased domestic diversity.

We struggled with one another (and still do sometimes), because the very issues we are exploring with participants are operating among us daily. This struggle doesn't always show up as race and gender issues. It can appear in differences of opinion over time boundaries, presentation content, or methodology.

I struggled with my role as leader of this diverse team. That is, sometimes my staff demanded more leadership and less leadership simultaneously, depending on the issues.

Participants in the Gender Forum often found it disappointingly less intense than the Multicultural Forum. There are several reasons for this: Some of the seasoned women were simply tired of discussing the same old issues with so little interest feeding back to them. Moreover, across the nation and in Purdue the majority of men and many of the younger women think that this issue is solved; and as women we are now in an era of individual responsibility, not group solidarity.

Though the subtext of sexism still existed in academia, there seemed to be no way to engage in meaningful cross-gender discussion. Bill Page, Barbara Berry, and I struggled for several years before we finally invented a design that facilitates both sexes engaging in enlightening conversation about current gender issues. The introduction of dialogue about LGBTQ issues has definitely enlivened, extended, and deepened this discussion.

Lesson 7. It is important to master current computer technologies to stimulate discussion and provide a change of pace, as people now expect powerful visuals for learning.

This lesson falls under Resistance for us. Only one of us was confident with new technologies, while the rest of us were in various stages of denial and distrust—touting the dynamic quality of overheads, flip charts, and the sterility of the screen, except for DVD and video. It took a number of years and a good amount of feedback from participants for us to even approach the skill level of the people in the forums. We are still learning.

Stage IV: Humility and Respect

Lesson 8. Accept, pursue, follow up, and act on feedback from participants.

Feedback opens the doors for innovation, new design, and deeper exploration by the consultants and attendees. Seeing the forums as a catalyst to broader culture change on campus, we hope that participants are empowered to be diversity champions in their own ways when returning to work.

Attending to negative feedback can provide an opportunity to defuse its power. Barbara Clark and I actively pursued negative feedback from the forums by listening and acting on the thoughts of others. Together we facilitated a large group session with the campus police when some felt they had been negatively stereotyped at a forum; in one college we sat with dissatisfied department heads to hear their thoughts and solicit their help in follow-up activities.

Lesson 9. To model a context of inclusiveness and colleagueship and to encourage deep learning, the consultants need to gradually share with participants their own journeys and vulnerabilities regarding diversity.

In the arenas of race, culture, and gender, none of us is fully aware or informed. However, it is not part of the academic culture to publicly share this kind of vulnerability. Academics are expected to be knowledgeable and they in turn expect their colleagues to be. Consultants do this, too.

We learned that we needed to be on guard against a kind of arrogance from pride in previous successes in other institutions. We do not always allow ourselves to be deeply touched by participants' life stories and struggles with these issues, especially those in the majority culture.

The consultants came to feel humbled by and to grow in admiration for the courage of so many people who opened themselves to challenging their beliefs, admitting in a large group the gaps in their knowledge and mistakes in their behavior. The forums deepen the humanity of the consultants as well as the participants.

This respect and admiration extends especially to the minority alumni, advanced students, and undergraduates whose intellectual and emotional honesty in sharing their campus experiences and afterthoughts provided in-depth learning and recommendations for change.

Looking forward, we believe all of the people involved in Purdue's work on inclusiveness have provided an innovative and solid foundation for President Cordova and Provost Woodson and others to lead the University toward their goals around student access and success. Our goal was to help shift the climate via new awareness and skills for faculty and staff so that new faculty and students would choose to join Purdue, present people would remain, and everyone would experience a greater sense of belonging.

ACKNOWLEDGEMENTS

Here are some of the people in my Purdue support system who have freely and frequently given of their time to be helpful to me and the diversity efforts. Please forgive me if I have left out any names:

In Engineering: Kathy Banks, Marian Blalock, Kamyar Haghighi, Klod Kokini, Leah Jamieson, Carolyn Percifield, Dick Schwartz, Linda Wang, Jeff Wright

In Science: Barbara Clark, Harry Morrison, Chris Sahley, Jeff Vitter

In Agriculture: Ron Coolbaugh, Joan Fulton, Rebecca Krisher, Vic Lechtenberg, Pam Morris, Suzanne Nielson, Dale Whittaker, Randy Woodson

In Consumer and Family Sciences: Thelma Snuggs, Rich Widdows

In Education: Nadine Dolby, Kevin Kelly

In Liberal Arts: John Contrini, Joan Marshall

In Pharmacy: Jackie Jimerson

In Technology: Denis Depew, Toni Munguia, Mary Sadowski

In Veterinary Medicine: Elikplimi (Eli) Asem

LGBTQ faculty and staff: Jim Gilligan, Kelly Leonard, Christopher Scott

LGBTQ student advocates: Kay Johnson, Christopher Munt, Alya Rahman, Lally Sothmann

The Provost's Diversity Leadership Group (DLG)

Provost Office and College of Science assistants and secretaries: Terri Donald, Paula Flores-Rojas, Becky Franklin, Janet Meade

Scores of others from the forums and from individual conversations have been companions along this important journey. I am grateful to all of you for your thoughts, for being my teachers, and for keeping the faith.

Thank you to the people at the Purdue Press for their interest and enthusiasm for this book and for their sure hands in guiding the editing and promotion.

And lastly, my enduring and heartfelt gratitude and admiration to my colleague, Barbara Benedict Bunker, who spent untold hours conducting interviews, checking facts, and doing rewrites to tell this story. Her patience with me and her unflagging energy for this project continue to inspire me.

NOTES

1. The research to create this narrative record involved interviews with 48 key stakeholders at Purdue: The provost, deans, faculty and staff, heads of departments, diversity directors, consulting staff and other key informants. The interview schedule is Appendix B. Evaluations of all the forums in the office of Barbara Clark, Special Assistant to the Provost, were examined. Materials used in the forums, reports written about the forums in articles, data from the Purdue University website, and other sources were reviewed. This research was approved by the Purdue University Human Subjects Review Committee IRB Protocol # 0702004913.

2.   As told by Deb Grubbe and others present at the meeting.

3.   www.science.purdue.edu/Diversity Forums/goals

4.   Driscoll, D.M., Kokini, K., Katehi, L..P..B., Wright, J..R., & Percifield, C..P. (2003). *A New Paradigm for Diversity in Engineering* In *Proceedings of the 2003 American Society for Engineering Education Annual Conference & Exposition.*

5.   Kelly, K. R., & Dolby, N. (2007). *Multicultural Forum Evaluation Final Report.* Purdue University: Department of Educational Studies.

6.   All quotes taken from handouts commonly used in the Gender Forum.

7.   Because participants now come to the Gender Forum from many colleges, the outcomes of this forum are individual rather than seen in the various colleges as documented in the Multicultural Forum or the early college retreats for women faculty.

8.   The Purdue University Data Digest, http://www.purdue.edu/DataDigest.

9.   *Chemistry and Engineering News* at http://pubs.acs.org/cen/education/83/pdf/8344womenacademia.pdf.

10.   See www.purdue.edu/provost/shtml/mosaic.shtml. Click *Mosaic* under *Related Links* to see the full text of the document.

11.   Mintzberg, H. (1979). *The Structuring of Organizations.* Englewood Cliffs, NJ: Prentice-Hall

12.   Diversity Assessment 2006-2007, Executive Report. Office of the Vice President for Human Relations, Purdue University.

13.   Shepard, Herbert A. (1975). "Rules of Thumb for Change Agents." The Organization Development Practitioner. November. pp. 1-5.

14.   Thanks to my colleague, Fritz Steele, for this term, which does not appear in consulting texts.

APPENDIX A

Category	Gender	Race	1997	1998	1999	2000	2001	2002	2003	2004	2005	2006
Academic, Assoc, Asst Deans	Men	White and Other	3	4	3	4	4	1	1	3	3	3
		Black	.	.	.	.	.	.	.	.	.	1
		Asian	.	.	.	.	2	2	2	2	2	1
	Women	White and Other	.	.	.	.	.	2	1	2	2	2
Academic Dept Heads	Men	American Indian	1	.	.	.	.	.	.	.	.	.
		White and Other	9	10	11	8	10	9	11	9	8	6
		Black	.	.	.	.	.	.	1	.	.	1
		Asian	.	.	.	.	.	.	.	1	1	.
		Hispanic	.	.	.	.	.	.	.	.	.	.
	Women	White and Other	1	1	1	1	1	1	.	1	1	2
Professors	Men	American Indian	.	1	1	1	1	1	.	1	1	1
		White and Other	100	99	96	100	97	96	94	101	103	100
		Asian	26	25	25	26	28	29	31	34	35	37
		Hispanic	1	1	1	1	1	2	2	2	2	3
	Women	White and Other	2	2	2	3	4	5	7	6	6	4
		Asian	1	1	1	1	2	2	2	3	4	4
		Hispanic	.	.	1	.	.	1	1	.	1	.
Associate Professors	Men	White and Other	60	57	50	49	47	47	47	51	59	56
		Black	.	.	.	1	1	2	2	2	2	2
		Asian	9	13	13	15	12	12	12	11	14	12
		Hispanic	2	3	3	2	2	1	2	2	2	2
	Women	White and Other	6	5	5	5	4	2	2	.	1	5
		Asian	2	2	3	3	4	4	5	4	3	2
Assistant Professors	Men	White and Other	26	29	25	29	25	25	26	24	25	20
		Black	1	.	.	.	.	1	1	1	2	2
		Asian	10	8	9	7	8	10	13	15	17	18
		Hispanic	1	1	.	.	.	.	.	3	3	3
	Women	White and Other	2	2	3	5	8	10	14	15	15	14
		Black	.	.	.	.	.	.	.	.	1	1
		Asian	3	4	3	2	2	2	1	1	3	3
		Hispanic	.	.	.	.	.	.	.	.	1	2
Grand Total			267	268	256	263	262	267	279	292	317	307

Table 1. College of Engineering

			1997	1998	1999	2000	2001	2002	2003	2004	2005	2006
Academic, Assoc, Asst Deans	Men	White and Other	2	2	2	3	2	3	2	3	2	2
	Women	Asian	.	1	.	.	.	1	2	1	1	1
Academic Dept Heads	Men	White and Other	5	5	5	4	4	3	3	4	5	5
		Asian	1	1	1	1	2	2	1	.	.	.
	Women	White and Other	1	1	1	1	2	2	2	2	.	.
Professors	Men	American Indian	.	.	.	.	.	.	.	.	.	.
		White and Other	150	147	151	144	138	137	134	127	125	122
		Black	2	2	2	2	2	2	2	2	2	2
		Asian	21	21	20	20	21	21	23	23	26	26
		Hispanic	3	3	4	5	5	5	5	5	4	4
	Women	White and Other	7	7	9	10	13	11	10	11	11	12
		Asian	2	2	1	1	1	2	2	2	1	2
Associate Professors	Men	American Indian	.	1	1	1	1	1	.	.	.	1
		White and Other	40	37	31	29	31	26	25	24	26	26
		Asian	5	6	6	5	6	8	10	10	12	12
		Hispanic	3	3	2	.	.	.	1	1	1	2
	Women	White and Other	10	9	7	8	8	6	4	5	6	7
		Asian	2	1	.	.	1	2	2	4	3	3
		Hispanic	.	.	.	.	1	.	.	.	.	3
		Asian	.	.	.	.	.	.	.	.	1	1
Assistant Professors	Men	American Indian	1	.	.	.	.	.	.	.	.	.
		White and Other	13	9	12	13	12	14	20	19	22	29
		Black	.	.	.	.	.	.	.	1	1	1
		Asian	6	6	8	10	10	12	14	16	21	20
		Hispanic	.	.	.	1	2	3	2	2	3	3
	Women	White and Other	5	7	6	7	7	8	11	10	11	12
		Asian	1	1	1	1	2	4	5	6	8	8
		Hispanic	1	1	1	2	2	4	5	6	8	8
Instructors	Women	White and Other	3	3	3	3	2	2	.	.	.	.
Grand Total			280	273	274	269	272	275	282	281	299	304

Table 2. College of Science

Table 3. College of Agriculture

			1997	1998	1999	2000	2001	2002	2003	2004	2005	2006
Academic, Assoc, Asst Deans	Men	White and Other	7	7	6	7	6	7	8	8	8	6
		Black	.	.	.	.	.	.	.	.	.	1
	Women	Asian	.	.	.	.	.	.	.	.	.	1
Academic Dept Heads	Men	White and Other	9	9	9	10	10	10	10	10	9	11
		Asian	1	1	.	.	.	.	.	.	.	.
	Women	White and Other	.	1	1	.	.	1	2	2	2	2
Professors	Men	White and Other	137	132	134	133	129	136	136	127	116	115
		Black	1	1	1	1	2	2	2	2	2	2
		Asian	7	7	7	7	6	7	8	10	10	10
		Hispanic	.	.	.	.	.	.	1	1	1	1
	Women	White and Other	10	10	9	10	12	12	12	12	14	17
		Asian	.	1	1	1	1	1	2	2	2	1
		Hispanic	.	.	.	.	.	1	1	.	.	.
Associate Professors	Men	White and Other	54	53	48	38	40	41	41	44	50	53
		Black	1	1	1	1	.	.	.	.	.	.
		Asian	2	3	4	4	4	5	4	4	6	6
		Hispanic	.	.	.	.	.	1	1	3	2	2
	Women	White and Other	7	8	8	11	11	11	13	14	13	13
		Black	.	.	.	.	.	.	1	1	1	.
		Asian	.	.	.	1	1	1	1	1	.	.
Assistant Professors	Men	White and Other	25	23	25	24	32	25	27	28	32	32
		Black	.	.	.	.	.	.	1	2	2	.
		Asian	3	4	3	3	4	3	4	4	6	8
		Hispanic	.	1	2	2	2	1	2	1	1	1
	Women	White and Other	9	8	11	10	10	11	14	14	12	12
		Black	.	1	1	1	2	2	1	2	2	2
		Asian	1	1	1	1	.	1	.	.	1	.
		Hispanic	.	.	.	.	.	.	.	.	1	1
Grand Total			275	272	273	265	273	278	289	290	292	299

APPENDIX B

Purdue Diversity Initiative

Interview Questions

1. How did you first get involved with the Diversity Initiative at
   Purdue?
   Please just tell me the story of your involvement.
2. Why did you become involved?
3. Who were the other people that were important in this initiative
   at that time?
4. Who supported this initiative? Has that changed over time?
   Was there opposition? Where? What happened?
   What was the role of the college/university leadership?
5. Did you attend one of the Multicultural Forums? Please tell me
   about that experience.
   How were the forums generally viewed? At the very
   beginning. Later?
6. Did you attend a Gender Forum? Please tell me about that
   experience.
7. What happened in your college as a result of the forums? (Is
   any of this documented? If yes, where?)
8. Are you a member of the Diversity Leadership Group? Please
   explain the work of this group at Purdue.
9. When you think about new initiatives that lead to change some
   things may happen easily and some may be difficult.
   Were there things that did happen easily (about any part of
   this initiative)?
   Was anything difficult or resisted?
10. Did anything happen in the university in general as a result
    of the forums or the Diversity Leadership Group (DLG),
    either positive, neutral, or negative?
11. Are there other people it is important that I talk to in order to
    get a true picture of the Diversity Initiative?
12. Is there any question that you think I should have asked that I
    didn't ask?